Endorsements for

"I have known Andy Park for decades. ... [a man] of high, unfeigned, unforced character—and right at the core of that godly character is humility. At this moment in history, we can hardly imagine any politician, actor, athlete or C-suite leader saying something like this: *"I am gentle and lowly in heart."* But Andy introduces us to such people. Jesus' life teaches us that humility is best cultivated by a bright "yes" to God, not a dark flagellating "no" to self. If you try it in the reverse, there is no context, no meaning and no goal for humility. Read *Living in Humility: Following the Humble King* and you'll discover both the kingdom-value of humility and guidance for pursuing it."

Bishop Todd Hunter, *pastor of Holy Trinity Anglican Church, Costa Mesa, California, and Author of: Our Character at Work*

"If anyone wants to follow a King whose first throne was a manger, a Holy One who touched lepers, a Master who spent some of his last hours on the floor washing feet, and a Savior lifted up at the end in scorn and derision, then read this book. Andy Park has created in this book an arena in which your heart will grapple with Scripture, saints, the Holy Spirit, and, ultimately, the One who is humility Incarnate."

Lester Ruth, *Research Professor of Christian Worship, Duke Divinity School, Durham, North Carolina*

"As the founder of a volunteer-based, inner-city outreach ministry, I have met thousands of people who humbly serve those around them – but none quite like Andy Park. As long as I've known Andy, he has put hands, feet and heart to the word "humility" in a way that is truly extraordinary. His book invites the reader into learning and living humility in a way that will change our own lives and the lives of those around us. Andy writes "...people will notice something special about you because you carry the traits of love and humility." That "something special" is why this book is must-read for me, my staff and the army of wonderful volunteers who serve at NightShift Street Ministries."

MaryAnne Connor, *Founder/President, NightShift Street Ministries*

Endorsements for *Living in Humility: Following the Humble King*

"One of the best things about this book is that it is written by someone who I have seen practicing the very issues he is writing about. Through Andy's vulnerability, the spirit of God used this book to challenge me in areas of leadership and character that I have let slip. Through personal accounts, relevant life stories of others and through good solid biblical teaching, Andy encourages us to develop a deep sense of this virtue that bears witness to who God is. I encourage you to read it reflectively and prayerfully."

Dr. Cameron Roxburgh, Senior Pastor, Southside Community Church, National Director, Forge Canada

"In his new book, "*Living in Humility: Following the Humble King* "Andy strikes a resonant chord that is wonderfully in tune with the character and invitation of Jesus. In all the noise and bluster of today's "hot-take" culture, this serves as a much needed call to return to the simple humility that is the Jesus way."

Kris MacQueen, *Vineyard Pastor & Songwriter, Creative Catalyst for Vineyard Canada*

Once I started reading *"Living in Humility: Following the Humble King,"* I didn't want to put the book down. The book is creative in its presentation and it not only challenges us intellectually with sound biblical teaching, but it invites us to examine our own hearts. Andy imparts so much wisdom as a spiritual father by making himself vulnerable to his readers. It's such an important book for the times in which we live and it's a must read.

Ruth Rousu, *former Pastor of Harvest Vineyard, Edmonton and National Team Member for Vineyard Canada*

Using stories and drawing on his own life experience, Andy paints a vivid picture of humility which confronts and attracts at the same time. On every page, we are reminded that being a follower of Jesus means enrollment in the perpetual school of humility. This book is an invitation to say yes to the counter-cultural way of Jesus in every area of our lives.

Matte Downey, *PhD, Pastor of Eglise Vineyard Montreal Church*

Living in Humility
Following the Humble King

Andy Park

Three Trees Publishing
©Andy Park, 2018
andypark.ca

Three Trees Publishing
www.andypark.ca
E-mail: info@andypark.ca

©2018 Andy Park

All rights reserved.

Scripture quotations marked (NIV) are taken from the Holy Bible, New International Version®, NIV®. Copyright © 1973, 1978, 1984, 2011 by Biblica, Inc.™ Used by permission of Zondervan. All rights reserved worldwide. www.zondervan.com The "NIV" and "New International Version" are trademarks registered in the United States Patent and Trademark Office by Biblica, Inc.™

Scripture quotations marked (NLT) are taken from the Holy Bible, New Living Translation, copyright ©1996, 2004, 2015 by Tyndale House Foundation. Used by permission of Tyndale House Publishers, Inc., Carol Stream, Illinois 60188. All rights reserved.

Scripture quotations marked MSG are taken from *THE MESSAGE*, copyright © 1993, 1994, 1995, 1996, 2000, 2001, 2002 by Eugene H. Peterson. Used by permission of NavPress. All rights reserved. Represented by Tyndale House Publishers, Inc.

Scripture quotations marked (CEV) are from the Contemporary English Version Copyright © 1991, 1992, 1995 by American Bible Society, Used by Permission.

Scriptures marked KJV are taken from the KING JAMES VERSION (KJV): KING JAMES VERSION, public domain.

Scripture quotations marked (ESV) are from The ESV® Bible (The Holy Bible, English Standard Version®), copyright © 2001 by Crossway, a publishing ministry of Good News Publishers. Used by permission. All rights reserved.

Scripture taken from the NEW AMERICAN STANDARD BIBLE®, Copyright ©1960, 1962, 1963, 1968, 1971, 1973, 1975, 1977, 1995 by The Lockman Foundation. Used by permission.

Every effort has been made to properly notate all references to published works. The author will be happy to rectify any omissions in future editions if notified by copyright holders.

This book is dedicated to
everyone from around the world
who is or wants to be
a sincere follower of Jesus,
our humble King

May you know
his unconditional love
and his empowering grace
as you follow him day by day

Stacey and Maitka

God bless you!

Andy Rak

Table of Contents

Chapter 1	Humility Personified	1
Chapter 2	The Good Soil of Humility	17
Chapter 3	Finding God in the Desert	25
Chapter 4	The Humble are Hungry for Righteousness	35
Chapter 5	A Teenage Girl Says Yes to God	45
Chapter 6	Doing, Seeing and Being Jesus	57
Chapter 7	Three Lives Poured Out	65
Chapter 8	Living for God's Approval	73
Chapter 9	Boast in the Lord	83
Chapter 10	Wait Patiently for the Lord	91
Chapter 11	Humility Wins Hearts	99
Chapter 12	Grace for Going to the Margins	109
Chapter 13	I Can't Believe You Said That!	117
Chapter 14	I Don't Like that Shade of White	125
Chapter 15	Be a Learning Machine	133
Chapter 16	Be a Team Player	139
Chapter 17	God is at Work in You	149
Chapter 18	Growing Older Graciously	157
Chapter 19	Staying on the Humble Path	167
Notes		172

Acknowledgements

I want to express my appreciation to all my friends who read this manuscript in its early and later stages and gave me valuable editorial input. It's a much better book because of the careful and wise observations of Karen White and Darcy White, Roy van der Westhuizen, Kris MacQueen, Matte Downey and Maryanne Connor. You have all given me insightful help!

Thanks to Gary Best for your encouragement to me go forward with this project. Also, thanks to Dev Randhawa for asking me the question in February of this year, "So, what are you doing to pass on your experience to the next generations?" That was the beginning point of pondering what I should do next, which led to writing this book.

Finally, a special thank to my very supportive wife, Linda, for her encouragement to me all throughout our marriage and in this project, to press on and give it all I've got.

1

Humility Personified

The word humility evokes various reactions from different people. William Bernard Ullathorne wrote: "The least known among the virtues and also the most misunderstood is the virtue of humility."[1]

When someone is described as *humble,* some people imagine a silly caricature: A quiet person, often looking down, unconfident, and very passive. He sighs a "woe is me, I'm just a worm" kind of attitude. He dresses in clothing 30 years out of date, never jokes around or does anything fun, and has a really boring personality.

This caricature of humility couldn't be farther from the truth. Humility isn't about demeaning yourself; it's not about being insecure, inadequate, or inferior to others. It's about embracing your God-given place in relation to Jesus and others.

Humility is the chief of the graces

Humility is not a personality type. It is a broad reaching orientation to all of life, towards God and people. Throughout history, many leading authors have identified humility as the most core virtue of following Jesus: The 19th century South African author and pastor, Andrew Murray, said: "The chief glory of heaven, the true heavenly-mindedness, the chief of the graces, is humility."[2] Thomas à Kempis wrote: "A true understanding and humble estimate of oneself is the highest and most valuable of all lessons."[3] Charles R. Swindoll once observed, "If I were to boil down all the characteristics of greatness to a single word, it would be humility."

There isn't a single area of life in which humility isn't required. To get through every single day in right relationship with God and people, I must take a humble posture before the Lord and others. In retrospect I can clearly see, "God stands against the proud, but favors the humble."[4] I don't want God to oppose me. I don't want God to stand against me. I want God's favor in my life!

James Johnson and Moses: Humility Personified

In the coming chapters, we will look at many people from all walks of life who can teach much us about humility. In all of Bible history, the only person who is called the "most humble" is Moses. People of many faith traditions have tremendous respect for Moses. He is clearly an exemplary figure. But it's not easy to put ourselves in Moses' shoes because of his unique and lofty position in ancient history.

What would a modern-day Moses look like? Consider this story of a first-world figure from the 20th century named James Johnson who has many Moses-like traits and experiences.

James Johnson was born in 1947 and grew up in a wealthy home in Atlanta, Georgia. He enjoyed all the privileges of an upper-class boy. His parents, Dennis and Sylvia Johnson, desperately loved him. This was partly because they couldn't have children of their own. Adopting James brought them great joy and fulfillment. Their joy was multiplied when his parents adopted two more children, Clarice and Jonas.

James' parents were Christians, and the family regularly attended church. On their 2-acre property was a tennis court, a basketball court, and all the toys the kids could want. They received the best care, food and education money could buy. James was a cheerful, generous boy, and an avid sportsman. People felt comfortable with James—he was a fun-loving, gentle soul and easily formed friendships. Early on, he rose to all-star status as a basketball player.

James played basketball for a private high school that saw his talent when he was only eleven years old. Beginning in the 8th grade James played with boys from all kinds of backgrounds and different parts of the city—both rich and poor. He developed very close friendships with a few of his teammates as the years went by. When it came to race, James didn't seem to see color. He was white and was equally comfortable with both black and white friends.

While traveling to games and hanging out at school, James was shocked to find out how poor some of his friends' families were. When James had some boys over to his house to hang out, he saw their amazement at his family's palatial home and property. His best friend, Marcus Wilson, a six-foot-nine forward who was raised by his single mother, told James stories of their poverty that made James' jaw drop.

James' parents were the owners of a network of businesses in the Atlanta area—hotels, restaurants, car washes and storage facilities. Dennis had inherited a few hotels from his parents and aggressively grew the business into a vast empire.

When it came time to think about a career, James had all kinds of options. He had an easy pathway towards a job in management with his dad's multitude of family businesses. A career in business wasn't the only option for James. College basketball recruiters were calling him, offering him full-ride scholarships to play ball at their schools. It was very attractive.

In July of 1963, in his sixteenth year, James had a deep, life-changing encounter with the Lord Jesus while at a youth conference. For the first time in his life, he *felt loved by* God. He had always believed in Jesus, but God seemed distant. After this amazing revelation of God's love, his

Living in Humility

former life seemed so shallow. Up until recently, all he ever thought about was himself—his plans, his future, his options. Now, his focus turned outwards. He had been given so much in life—loving parents, a great upbringing and plenty of resources. How could he give back?

One month after James' life-changing encounter with the Holy Spirit, there was another pivotal moment in his life. He listened to Martin Luther King deliver his "I Have A Dream" speech at the "March on Washington for Jobs and Freedom" on August 28.

In the speech, King referred to the Emancipation Proclamation of 1863 by which millions of slaves were freed. He loudly proclaimed to the huge audience of 250,000 from the steps of the Lincoln Memorial: "one hundred years later, the Negro still is not free." King's dream was for freedom and equality to replace the bigotry and hatred that still prevailed in the hearts and actions of many Americans.

The speech gripped James Johnson. He was riveted by every word spoken by Dr. King. In the following week, James had his own dream while fast asleep. He saw a series of scenes in which he was conversing with a variety of young adults, both Caucasian and African American. He saw himself speaking words of encouragement and instruction to these young people. He awoke and could remember the pained expressions on the faces of these young adults. There was a sense of destiny about the dream. He didn't have a clear interpretation of the dream's meaning, but it seemed like another piece in the puzzle of his future.

As he spent time with God over the next year, a deep sense of calling began to rise up in him. He wanted to share the wealth of God's love somehow. He began by gathering his buddy, Marcus, and a few of his other teammates to put on some free basketball clinics for elementary school kids in low-income neighborhoods. They had a great time and saw how much the kids appreciated the attention and training. James thought, "This is just the beginning."

As James went deeper into knowing the Lord, God began to unearth some of his past memories, hurts and sins. James began to wonder who his birth parents were. His adoptive parents had never given him any details about his origins. When James pressed his parents on this subject, they were reluctant to give him any more information. But they realized they couldn't hide it from him. So, they told him the truth—his biological mother was a young woman who got caught up in a teenage love affair. She was much too young to care for a child, so she put James up for adoption.

James went through the process of finding his birth mom and arranged to meet her. She was a sweet woman named Caroline who came from a little rural town in the northeast corner of Georgia. As they sat together over a cup of coffee, Caroline told James the story of growing up in poverty, falling in love with a young man and getting pregnant in her teens. When James saw the simple home of his birth mother, he looked at his privileged life through new eyes.

In the weeks after that reunion with his birth mother, wave after wave of God's invitation to service came washing over James. He didn't feel especially gifted to lead others, but he couldn't deny the success he had in rallying a group of his peers to reach out to younger boys. Part of him wanted to push away these signals that seemed to be from God and pursue a career in professional sports. At the same time, he wanted to help people that *really needed help*. He want to help people like his birth mom, and his teammates whose families barely had two nickels to rub together.

By now, it was 1965, and the civil rights movement had come to a boil. That spring, around 600 civil rights workers marched in Alabama to protest black voter suppression. More and more, James was gripped with the shameful inequities he saw in society. James couldn't escape the tugging on his heart to help poor families, no matter what color they were.

Living in Humility

After more months of prayer and advice from his pastors, he decided he would study sociology and play basketball at the nearby University of Georgia. He would also study historical issues of social justice. His parents couldn't understand why he would want to study sociology when the door to the family business was wide open, but they let him go ahead. He began to understand that his life was about pleasing God, not people. As much he loved his parents, he wanted God's best choice for his life.

During his busy college years, he made time to run more basketball camps, and mentor some young basketball players from his training camps – sharing his faith with them and giving them practical advice on moving forward in their relationships and studies. It dawned on him that this is how to change the world—one conversation at a time.

During one of his basketball camps, James made one of the biggest mistakes of his life. In the last session, the boys were in a full-court scrimmage. This was their last chance to impress the coaches. The boys' pride was on the line. At times it looked more like a football game with all the heavy physical contact. Tempers were flaring and in the 3rd quarter, a fight broke out when two players got tangled up in the key.

Sam Campbell, a head-strong white boy who was knocked down in the collision, started screaming racial insults at Darius Brown, a black player. James immediately stepped in and tried to break up the fight. Instead of backing down, Sam kept on screaming in a rage, "you dirty nigger..." Before he knew what he was doing, James slugged Sam in the face, knocking him to the floor.

James felt terrible about his violent reaction and apologized to Sam right away. He wrote a letter of apology to Sam and his father and offered to pay for any medical expenses from the fight. He waited anxiously to see if Sam's dad would file a lawsuit, but nothing came of it.

James' explosion of anger showed him how much he hated racial discrimination. His close friendship with Marcus Wilson and seeing news reports of the terrible clash between whites and blacks in the southern U.S. had made him feel protective of African-Americans. But he also saw that he really had to deal with his anger issue.

Towards the end of his undergraduate studies, James continued to agonize over the decision of what to do next. After achieving all-star status in his 4-years of college ball, his basketball coaches kept telling him he had a chance to get drafted by a professional team. But he didn't know if he should hang onto that dream. "Not my will, but yours be done," was his frequent prayer.

He kept wondering if he should become a lawyer who could help those who had no power, no voice and no way to protect themselves or their families. It could be a way of defending the needy and also fighting for reform in laws that discriminated against non-whites. He had badly misused his zeal for racial harmony in the incident with Sam Campbell. But, maybe he could turn a corner and use that energy in a positive way.

James didn't know if he had the right stuff to be good lawyer. He wasn't aggressive or confrontational or super articulate. But he knew how to work hard. Waiting quietly before the Lord one day, he felt God say, "I am with you...can you just trust me with childlike faith?" After months of waiting, listening and praying James took the leap to study law. His parents were happy about his ambitions to study law, but skeptical about the social justice part of the plan.

Ten years later, James took a job at a small law firm in Atlanta specializing in workers rights and doing pro-bono work for those who couldn't afford legal aid. With his soft-spoken, gentle personality, he found it hard to be firm with people who needed to break their bad habits. But he was gradually growing in confidence. He depended on God's help for every meeting with a client and every courtroom appearance.

Living in Humility

James had many clients who came from dysfunctional families. These families produced some irresponsible, immature young adults who brought their issues into James' office. It took incredible patience and perseverance to lead these young men and women towards responsible behavior.

James often thought, "What have I gotten myself into?" Many of James' clients complained bitterly about their lot in life. Some of them were full of self-pity and excuses. They had trouble holding down a job. They hadn't grown up with parents who could set an example of working steadily. For his first several years as a young attorney, he made little money, and got little respect from his clients. He had to let go of the right to be appreciated. There was no immediate pay-off in this line of work.

James often felt like throwing up his hands and quitting the whole business. He got discouraged, but he never quit. He knew that quitting would be walking away from God's calling. Sure, he could bail out on practicing law and take the easy road of joining the family business. But he knew it would be a choice he would regret. God had made it so clear that this was the right path.

For many years, his family had questioned his desire to go into social justice work. They argued with him, "You're working long hours and the money isn't good." Aside from that, they made the occasional comment revealing their prejudice towards blacks. His parents kept dropping hints about joining the family business. They couldn't accept his choice to serve the "lower class" folks in town. They heaped praise on his younger siblings, who were both working in the family business.

James had never imagined that his love for the same God his parents worshiped would create a huge rift between them. He was the son of Dennis and Sylvia, but he felt like he had to choose between pleasing his earthly parents and his heavenly Father. Visiting his family home had become awkward for James. He felt almost like an outcast among his own family.

He occasionally got angry at his family's comments and lashed out at them, accusing them of ignoring the needs of the poor. Once in awhile, James' zeal was tainted with anger and judgment. One time, he confronted his father on his poor treatment of low-level employees. That caused a falling-out, and a period of silence between father and son. But James came around and owned his mistake and apologized, asking for forgiveness.

James' sister Clarice was especially tough on James, mocking him for rejecting the obvious right choice of following in his father's footsteps in the family business. When she developed a cancerous tumor in her mid-twenties, James was there to pray for her and comfort her. He rejoiced to see her healed and restored to full health.

At the age of 29, James married his long-time sweetheart, Jody Williams. Jody came from a non-Christian family, which made things tricky at times. Jody's father, Cody, was also a lawyer. James was put off by some of Cody's language and behavior, but he was open-minded and accepting towards his new in-law. With a common law profession, the two had a lot to talk about.

Year by year, he kept leading his young clients into responsible living, teaching them basic things like forgiveness, kindness and loving your enemy. In his 30's, James' perseverance was bearing more fruit. Slowly but surely, he was being transformed into a very capable leader. His law practice was growing quickly and the firm was hiring more and more attorneys, some of whom worked in James' department. James was promoted to partner status in the company, and with it came managerial responsibility.

As James found himself overwhelmed with his case load, his father-in-law, Cody offered some valuable advice on how to manage his business.

Living in Humility

James was quick to listen and benefited from Cody's knowledge. He made the wise decision of listening to Cody even though he wasn't a Christian and specialized in a different area of law.

Over the next eight years, wonderful things were happening in James' work. He had spent 18 years helping young offenders get reduced prison sentences, defending young widows, and helping some of them find steady employment. James' parents saw the fruit of his labors and had a change of heart. No longer did they criticize his work. Instead, they saw the tremendous value of their son's work and began to talk about different ways of partnering with him.

His father asked him, "How about starting sports clubs that will help these kids get off the streets at a young age? How about offering scholarships to some of our top-performing young employees who can't afford to go to college?" Clarice joined in with her own ideas about starting a mentoring program for teenage girls in low income neighborhoods of the greater Atlanta area.

One thing led to another, and the elder Johnsons got behind the vision with their considerable cash reserves. They used their connections in the city to recruit more donors and workers. James' reputation as a lawyer had blossomed in the Atlanta area. He used his influence to recruit workers from all over the city for the new programs. Within a year, the word spread all over Atlanta and beyond about all of the projects under James Johnson's name, and the media began to cover it. Before you knew it, James became a local hero, and people were suggesting he run for political office.

It seemed that God was showing great favor to James, after all those years of slugging away, case by case with needy, broken people. When James said yes to God's call, it was a slow road of learning, serving and growth. But in the long run of time, amazing miracles happened. Thousands of needy people were helped and many leaders from all over the United States took notice and started similar programs in their communities.

Even with the impressive success and notoriety, James never got a big head. He always had a healthy sense of his own limitations. He knew God had air-lifted him out of poverty and had given him an amazing start in life. His early years of slowly plodding ahead as a young lawyer were forever etched into his memory. He needed God then, and he was still totally dependent on God's help.

When people were singing his praises, he didn't settle back and let the young guys do all the work. He wasn't finished learning, growing and going for God. He kept asking God for more blessing, more strength, and more vision for the next steps. He wasn't living in the past. He was pressing on towards the future, eagerly asking God to be with him. He didn't see himself as having "arrived" as a great leader. He knew it was all because of God's grace. He humbly kept going, asking God for wisdom for the next steps.

James and Moses have "most humble" traits

You may or may not have guessed that James Johnson is a fictional character. My purpose in creating James' story was to bring alive the very same traits we see in the life of Moses, showing us *why* Moses was called "the most humble man on earth." I think most of us find it easier to see something of ourselves in a 20th century character like James than in the incomparable Moses, who could turn his staff into a serpent and bring forth water from a rock.

The lives of both James and Moses are great examples of practical humility in all areas of life. Humility shaped their attitudes, ambitions, the way they related to God and the way they dealt with people.

James was **unassuming and unambitious**, just like Moses. They were both very reluctant to respond to God's call to become liberators of the oppressed, with an attitude of, "Who am I to do such a thing?" They both lacked confidence as they first launched out but hung onto God and took the right steps. That's humility: "God, I'm weak. Please be my strength as I step out in faith."

God **supernaturally called** Moses and James to be liberators of the oppressed. For Moses, the revelations came through the burning bush experience and numerous one-on-one conversations with God. James received his calling through various personal encounters with God and through more natural means, like getting advice from friends. He received a steadily growing conviction that he must choose a career path to help the needy, and he had one very clear divine dream. Both Moses and James were faithful to the clear messages they received from God. That's an expression of humility—"God, I bow to your choice for my life."

James and Moses were both **raised in wealthy families,** but their real family roots were on the other side of the tracks. They both left behind their privileged positions to become liberators of the oppressed. They identified with people who had much less power and resources than they did.

While Moses' adoptive father was a tyrannical ruler, James' dad was a Christian who couldn't see the value of lifting up the poor. James is torn by this conflict, but in the end chooses to please God instead of people. He takes a radical step *away from* his earthly family to answer a call to reach across a racial and economic boundary line. Again, he prefers God's choice over personal comfort.

Moses shepherded a very large group of unruly, complaining people. He put up with their forgetfulness of God's many miraculous interventions. When there wasn't good water to drink or food to eat, they complained. Most of the time, Moses was patient with his grumbling flock. On many occasions, Moses was very frustrated with his people, but he never deserted them. He faithfully and humbly served them. James had a similar track record in his work with his complaining clients. **Humility is to bear with the failings of the weak.**

Both **Moses and James had problems with anger** and acted out violently. James didn't commit murder like Moses did, but he violently attacked another person and learned a valuable lesson in the process. He didn't let his mistakes define him; instead, he overcame his violent temper.

Moses was merciful to his sometimes wayward flock. He appealed to God on behalf of his people, even when they worshiped the golden calf. James showed the same kind of patience with his immature, self-centered clients.

In many ways, their situations were vastly different. But, both James and Moses were called by God to do something they did not choose. On many occasions, they both felt like quitting the impossible assignment God gave them, but they stuck with it. They didn't walk away from their calling. **To persevere in a lifetime of service requires humility.** Humility is cooperating with God, in the big and small decisions of life, even when the going gets really tough.

It takes to humility to walk in a long obedience in the same direction like Moses and James did. Whether you're teaching school children, pastoring a church, or building homes, it's a long marathon we run. In serving the people around us day-by-day, we are serving our Master, Jesus.

Even when Moses' brother and sister turned against him by publicly complaining against him for marrying a foreign wife, he showed compassion. Moses was merciful to Aaron and Miriam, asking the Lord to heal them of leprosy. James did the same for his sister, Clarice, despite her hostile opposition to his life choices. Though he chafed against his parents' values and choices, he didn't cut them out of his life.

Moses' **humility was first expressed in surrender**, and later expressed in using his authority to release God's saving power through signs and wonders. The order of those two things is key. First surrender, then came

Living in Humility

works of power. James didn't part the Red Sea, but he experienced a similar progression. A couple decades into his career, his good influence and reputation had spread far and wide because of God's favor and his stubborn perseverance.

James stayed humble, even after rising to prominence, just like Moses, who had no illusions about the limitations of his own power. Moses carried a sobering responsibility—leading a small nation to freedom. He knew it was way above any human's ability level. James had the same attitude. He remained "small in his own eyes."

Another way James paralleled the life of Moses was by listening to his father-in-law, an older man with a different spiritual orientation. Moses' father-in-law, Jethro, was a "priest of Midian," and prior to meeting Moses, had not worshipped Yahweh, the God of Israel. Despite Jethro's background of worshiping other gods, Moses listened to this newcomer for advice. **A key mark of humility is being open to input from all kinds of people.** All wisdom is God's wisdom, no matter who speaks it.

Moses' father-in-law advised him to recruit leaders who would help him carry the heavy load of leading a massive group of people. This was incredibly valuable information for Moses, who was responsible for over a million people. Moses humbly respected his elder in-law. James showed the same readiness to listen and learn from a more experienced man even after proving his competence as a young attorney.

Neither of these men ever saw themselves as having "arrived." After God used Moses in the amazing episodes of the Red Sea, the golden calf, and all the many signs and wonders, Moses kept asking God for more blessing, more favor, and more revelation of his goodness. He continued asking God to teach him his ways, and to bring his presence wherever he went.

James took a similar approach. He wasn't living in the past, patting himself on the back for his success. He was pressing on towards the future, eagerly asking God to be with him. He wasn't finished learning, growing and going for God. He humbly kept going, step by step, in dependence on God all the way.

Examples of humility from every era and occupation

In the chapters to come, we will look at dozens of notable people who lived in humility. (James is our only fictitious character!). From professional athletes to CEO's to early church fathers, to typical moms and dads and single people, to monks and nuns, we hear the call to live in humility as we follow the humble King.

2

The Good Soil of Humility

Seek Jesus, find humility
Should the focus of our life's pursuit be *humility*? No, *Jesus* is our focus. At the core of Jesus' nature is humility. He will lead us into taking on his nature.

Jesus humbled himself to the very lowest place and as a result was exalted to the very highest place. In Jesus, a very important spiritual principle is demonstrated: those who humble themselves will be lifted up—honored or exalted. Jesus followed the Father's plan and was rewarded with the very highest honor of any human in history.

Jesus shows us the definition of humility – saying "yes" to his loving Father's plan. He cooperated with his Father, saying "not my will, but yours be done." To be a disciple of someone is to copy everything they do. It's to absorb and become everything they are. Being apprenticed to Jesus means taking on his character. Because humility is central to the character of Jesus, by seeking him, you enroll in his school of humility.

When a new position becomes available in your company and you see yourself as highly qualified for that position, but someone else gets promoted, God is taking you to humility school. When you passionately argue your point with a friend but in the end, you see she is right and you are wrong, and you admit it, you're learning humility.

When your role at work is discontinued and it seems like God has pulled the carpet out from under you, you feel like asking "Have I done something wrong?" Not necessarily. It means: It's time to grow!! God is saying, "I'm pruning you, purifying you, getting you ready for the next step." You are God's child and you're also his student. What a privilege—to follow in his footsteps, humbly serving just as he did. This is the key to life, happiness and fulfillment.

Good Soil
When I plant flowers in a pot or a tree in the ground, I make sure I am using healthy soil. Without a nutritious environment, the plant won't grow. In becoming a student of Jesus, we develop the "good soil" of humility. *Humility creates an environment in which Christ-like qualities can thrive and grow.* Humility is the soil in which my *trust in God* can grow. When my life seems to be falling apart, I must humble myself to trust a higher being. I must humbly surrender the right to understand why God allows injustice and suffering. Without humility, I can't yield to God in the tests and trials of life.

A humble attitude equips you to handle the big questions of life. With humility, you can accept how God uniquely made you and those around you. With humility, you can believe in a God you don't fully understand. With humility, you can fulfill your God-given potential, even if you end up doing something you didn't choose.

Humility is the soil in which *love* grows:
Love is patient.   The proud must be first, while the humble wait for others.
Love is kind.   The proud are often too self-occupied to be kind.
Love is not jealous.   The humble are thankful for what they have and content to be just who they are; they resist jealous impulses.

Love is not boastful. The humble don't boast because they recognize their gifts, abilities and accomplishments are gifts from God.

Humility is the soil in which *gratitude* grows. Humility acknowledges God as the giver of every good gift. Albert Einstein said, "There are only two ways to live your life. One is as though nothing is a miracle. The other is as though everything is a miracle."

Interdependent Traits

In 2012, Jordan LaBouff of the University of Maine conducted a study on humility. His findings support the humility-as-good-soil idea. Here are a few results from his study: Humble friends are more loyal than prideful ones. "Compassion is hard if you don't have humility," says LaBouff.[5]

In one of LaBouff's experiments involving 117 college students, various personality traits were measured. "The researchers found that of all the personality traits measured, humility was the most strongly linked with helpfulness."[6]

Without humility...
    Without humility, I can't be thankful when life beats me up.
    Without humility, I can't forgive when I'm insulted or disrespected.
    Without humility, I can't volunteer my time to serve someone who has no way of paying me back.
    Without humility, I can't shut up and listen to my wife's side of an argument.
    Without humility, I can't graciously bend with the changing seasons and responsibilities of my life.

This list goes on and on. Without humility, you can't surrender your power over people and situations. Without humility, you can't lay down your own agenda and let the Holy Spirit lead you. Without humility, you can't obey God when you don't feel like it.

God enables the humble to accomplish the tasks he gives them. The apostle Paul spoke of the enabling grace of God that helped him work hard. "I have worked harder than all the other apostles...yet it was not I but God who was working through me by his grace."[7] God's grace was given to empower Paul, when he was weakened by his "thorn in the flesh." He received this grace by humbling himself to the Lord.

If you're smart, you'll learn humility. If you want your relationship with God to flourish, you'll walk humbly. If you want satisfying relationships with your family, friends and work mates, you'll develop a humble heart. If you want the best long-term rewards available, you'll always be learning from Jesus' example of humility.

Humility is a safeguard against unnecessary failure and disappointment. We will make mistakes and be disappointed, but we can minimize that by learning the Jesus way. Humility makes us ready to learn from anyone, anywhere, anytime. Without humility, you can't be a lifelong learner. To be an apprentice of Jesus we must constantly have the humility of a child who is eager to learn. A teachable heart opens the door to God's grace.

Humility brings rewards
Scripture teaches that we catch God's attention by walking in humility. Despite the trials we may undergo, walking in humility brings a huge reward:
When pride comes, then comes disgrace,
but with the humble is wisdom.[8]
God saves and shows favor to the humble.[9]
God guides and sustains the humble.[10]
He crowns the humble with victory [11]
He hears the prayers of the humble.[12]
Humility is the fear of the LORD; its wages are riches and honor and life.[13]

The Good Soil of Humility

The God of all grace is *all about* helping us, enabling us, and blessing us. The idea of *grace* in the Bible describes the whole of God's activity towards his children. It's available in unlimited measure to those who choose a humble path. Andrew Murray says in his book Humility: "Here is the path to the higher life: down, lower down! Just as water always seeks and fills the lowest place, so the moment God finds men abased and empty, His glory and power flow in to exalt and to bless."[14]

Learning from our mistakes

Our actions have consequences. You'll be blessed if you walk humbly. You'll lose out if you're proud. I've done plenty of both. If I insist on my own way in church leadership, I will lose favor with my co-workers. Nobody wants to work with a selfish tyrant. If I criticize my wife, I immediately lose out. She shuts down in conversation because I've built a wall between us.

Sometimes I've done it right. Like the times I've reconciled with my wife after saying something rash and hurtful. And the times I've kept my mouth shut when I could have spoken critically. And the times I've passed over the mistakes of other people even when it hurt me.

And sometimes I've done it wrong—making hurried decisions based on my ideas instead of God's plans. I've run ahead to start a new project instead of humbly waiting for God's timing. I later paid the consequences. In my marriage, my work and friendships, I'm sunk if I don't walk humbly. I've learned this lesson many times by letting pride and self-centeredness rule me instead of a humble heart.

Humble achievers

Many people throughout history accomplished great things because they said "yes" to being small in comparison to God's grandeur. Small in wisdom compared to God's omniscience. Small in authority compared to God's omnipotence. That's humility.

When Paul, an ambitious Pharisee, humbled himself to Jesus' call, he planted churches throughout the ancient Near East and wrote letters that would comprise the majority of our biblical New Testament. God poured out his grace. When Peter, a loud-mouthed fisherman, humbled himself to Jesus' invitation to "feed his sheep," he led thousands to Christ and was one of the primary leaders of the earliest Christian churches. God poured out his grace.

Personalities from biblical times like Moses, Paul and Jesus show us the attitudes, behaviors and blessings of walking in humility. All the resources of God are available to the humble: strength, courage, wisdom, and more. This is the path to a successful life—God's definition of success.

When you and I humble ourselves to God's call, he places us in all sectors of society—our own homes, business, education, service industries and more—to reflect his nature. God pours out his grace as we work with humble confidence.

A Lifelong Process
Looking back over the years, I can see I've found contentment when I've chosen a humble path. Humbling myself to God and others is why I am still in the game—still loving God, serving people and growing in wisdom. I can think of plenty of friends who have fallen off the wagon because they didn't choose the humble road.

Humility is God's plan for you. He made you to know him and be like him; he is the humble King. He is eager to pour out his grace on you. Jesus said, "Let me teach you, because I am humble and gentle at heart, and you will find rest for your souls."[15] In finding Jesus, the humble King, you rest from striving to be something you're not. You receive his grace for your everyday work and relationships.

In the humble life, you get the satisfaction of knowing you are great in God's eyes, no matter what your position, job, income or status in the world is. Humility is foundational for us all. It touches every single aspect of life. It's the core of who Jesus is, and who he calls us to be. A humble attitude paves the way for easy interaction with all kinds of people.

Humility is central to the Christian life
I've written a book on humility not because I consider myself an expert on the subject. I've written on it because I'm seeing how central it is to following Jesus. Early this year, a friend challenged me, "what are you doing to give away your wisdom and experience to the next generations?" After much thought and prayer, I decided to write this book. For the past few years, *humility* has been the number one theme God has been teaching me. I am constantly learning and growing. The more I've thought about it, the more I'm convinced that it's one of the most crucial issues we wrestle with. Along with "love God and neighbor," humility is one of the most important, all-pervasive character qualities God develops in us as we seek to keep growing.

I still have a long way to go as a student of Jesus. My heart isn't fully trained and tamed like it needs to be. I've made a lot of progress but I still have ego problems. I'm not worried because he is very patient with me. Thank God for his endless grace! God is faithful to complete the work he starts in us. His immeasurable grace is available for those who walk the humble road.

Andrew Murray on Jesus' humility: "His chief characteristic, the root and essence of all His character...is His humility. What is the incarnation but His heavenly humility, His emptying Himself and becoming man? What is His life on earth but humility; His taking the form of a servant? And what is His atonement but humility?"[16]

3

Finding God in the Desert

A shy 17-year old kid finds God's love, picks up a guitar, writes and sings worship songs in his church. A few years into it, he is driving around Los Angeles to do concerts and lead worship in different churches. About 10 years in, his travels extend around the world. He begins recording CDs, and some of his songs become internationally known. Over the next 15 years, he continues recording and gradually earns enough money from his music to feed his family of ten. In another 5 years, everything begins to slow down—less invitations to lead worship, less travel, less recording, and much less income. God says, "let go of everything."

If you guessed it's me I'm describing, you're right. For around 20 years, I played on big stages, traveled to over 30 nations, and recorded dozens of worship albums. Since then, the audiences are smaller, the travel has decreased and the recordings are now done in my own home studio. I'm still ministering regularly, writing lots of songs and traveling to various places. But there is much less fanfare and hoopla.

This transition was gradual, which made it an easier adjustment. But I can't say it was easy. Brent Rue, a Vineyard pastor who died early in life, and traveled to many nations to speak, said, "When I come home, people treat me like 'white bread.'"

Living in Humility

"White bread" is boring, tasteless and the last thing I want to eat, or to be. I know exactly what Brent was talking about. People treat you like royalty when you're the guest speaker in a far away land, but they almost ignore you at home. Another Vineyard pastor used to say, "When I get home from doing a ministry trip where lots of people were healed, I come home and my wife says, "Can you take out the garbage?"

Taking out the garbage is *really good* for our humility level! It's *exactly* the kind of thing Jesus was doing when he washed the disciples' feet. Those streets of Galilee were filled with animal dung and all kinds of nasty stuff. Jesus wasn't doing some kind of ceremonial thing when he washed his friends' feet. He was getting the filth off!

For me, it was a test to get *onto* the big platforms, and a test to get *off* them. Was I willing to accept my new, less impressive job description from God? Or was I going to insist on having things "like they used to be?" Tuning in to the Holy Spirit, I navigated through all these twists and turns. And in the process I think I'm slowly becoming a little more like Jesus. That's the whole point, isn't it?

The next season of life
After much reflecting, soul searching and more than a little repenting and anguish, I'm finding a lot of peace and fulfillment these days. It's a really good time of life! I'm catching the big picture God has for me—serve wherever you have the opportunity. It's the oldest lesson in the book.

I've let go of my expectations of what my ministry will look like. I'm happy serving regardless of the rewards, the respect, or the venue. Much of my work is unpaid volunteer work. And I'm content. God's grace is poured out.

My family's needs are met and I'm doing what I've always done, but it comes in a different package. After 27 years of raising children, my wife now works as a midwife. Linda cares for pregnant moms and delivers babies. Her income pays most of the bills! Hallelujah, glory. I didn't see that one coming, but God did.

A word of wisdom from Richard Rohr: "All great spirituality teaches about letting go of what you don't need and who you are not. Then, when you can get little enough, you'll find that the little place where you really are is more than enough and is all that you need... That place is called freedom."[17]

When Moses fled from Pharaoh's clutches after killing an Egyptian, he found himself in the desert. It was a place of letting go.

"Moses remained in a solitary, non-public existence for a long time. It was as if—in some deep and fundamental way—he just let go. He let go of his dreams of fixing anything, helping anyone or even living among his people. Instead he received what was given."[18]

Of course, that wasn't the end of the story for Moses. But there had to be a letting go before there was a moving forward. I've found great freedom in letting go of any attitude of entitlement. The small place is a good place. You find God and his love there. You get what you need from him. I have nothing to prove to anyone and no need to protect my reputation. Life is easier when I humbly accept the cards God is dealing out to me.

This is how God designed us to live. Happily taking the next job assignment God gives us, even if it looks very different than the previous one. It's the happy downward journey Jesus models for us and invites us to take with him: "...in humility value others above yourselves, not looking to your own interests but each of you to the interests of the others..."[19]

Jesus let go of his power, privilege and position as God to become a lowly human. In letting go of privileges I used to enjoy, I've found that He is with me, speaking to me, leading me. I'm happy as long as I keep letting go.

Living in Humility

I look at my past few years as a type of desert experience. God has tested me. He has taken some things away from me, and I have chosen not to hang on to those things. Instead, I am hanging onto Him and I've found peace and contentment.

The Father took Jesus to the desert

Jesus is the forerunner for all believers—the Father led him into the desert to test and try him. When Jesus was baptized, the Spirit of God descended "like a dove" on him. A voice from heaven said, "This is my Son, whom I love; with him I am well pleased."[20]

In the very next verse, we read: "Then Jesus was *led by the Spirit* into the wilderness to be *tempted* by the devil." At the baptism, the Father essentially tells Jesus: "I am so proud of you!" Though Jesus had not yet done any public ministry, the Father affirms how pleased he is with his son. The *very next thing* the Father does is to take Jesus to the desert to *test him*! This is what our Father does with all of us. He refines our faith and character through trials and temptations. He teaches us to surrender our power.

Jesus' desert experience is a model for us. The context is this: God loves you and is inviting you to go deeper with him. When he takes you to the desert, it doesn't mean you've done anything wrong! He is testing your character. In the desert, who we are is revealed. He refines us. We go deeper in trusting him. We humble ourselves to learn whatever it is he's trying to teach us. He gives us grace to endure difficulty and become more like him.

> This is how Paul describes his own agonizing desert experience: "We do not want you to be uninformed, brothers and sisters, about the troubles we experienced in the province of Asia. We were under great pressure, far beyond our ability to endure, so that we despaired of life itself. Indeed, we felt we had received the sentence of death."[21]

Paul had great insight—he saw that God's reason for putting him under unbearable pressure was to increase his reliance on God. Paul sees God behind the scenes of this desert time, so he writes, "But this happened that we might not rely on ourselves but on God, who raises the dead."[22]

God purposely humbles us

Why does he humble us? So that we can know him better, rely on him more, and make less mistakes in the future. The journey to the promised land always goes through the desert. God purposely humbles us to teach us his ways. Every person who sincerely follows Jesus should get ready to embrace humbling experiences. It's part of God's game plan.[23]

Get ready to be offended, demoted, and disregarded. Get ready to be hurt so you can learn to forgive. Get ready to be stumped by life's big questions so you can learn to trust. Get ready to try your hardest and fail so you can learn to trust God and get back up and try again. How else are we going to learn humility, and learn to trust him? Only in difficulty are we forced to grow. Otherwise, we coast down the hill. When we hike *up* the steep hill, God gets our attention.

God *made you* to be like him. God is humble. Ready to go to humility school? People who want to follow God are required to go to the desert. The idea of "desert" or "wilderness," speaks of God's tests and trials in our lives. In the desert, things in life that support us are *taken away.* In Jesus' desert temptation, food and friends were taken away for a season. He was alone and hungry.

All Jesus-followers must do some laps in the desert. There is no one in the whole story of the scriptures who doesn't have to go to the desert. Our forefathers all spent some time in the desert or wilderness. Abraham, Jacob, Moses, Ruth, Elijah, and Mary were there. Their examples guide us as we also pass through the wilderness.[24]

God's plan was to compel Jesus out into the desert to shape his life and ministry. "Jesus has to learn how to say "no" to the devil in order to say "yes" to the Father. All of us must learn these same lessons."[25]

God speaks to us in the desert. In Hebrew, the word for wilderness is *midbar*. The root of *midbar* has the meaning of "speak" or "word." God speaks to us in the wilderness. God shows great compassion to those in the desert. In our intensified need for him, we become better listeners. Your desert experience could be a job that is taken away, or a ministry, or a relationship. It feels like things are falling apart. You have to lean on God more than ever.

As I look back on the last four decades, I remember many desert experiences, some short, some longer and more difficult. I've faced all kinds of things in the desert: troubles with my finances, my job, my ministry, a relationship, and dealing with a difficult boss. Throughout my 30's and 40's, God blessed me in a thousand ways. But he continued to train me with many hard lessons. Being treated unjustly by certain leaders and friends challenged me to forgive and bless those who mistreated me. My struggle to rightly handle conflict with others brought me to my knees.

God leads us into the desert and takes away (or he allows the enemy to take away) whatever wall we're leaning against so we can depend on him, know him, trust him, worship him. You don't know what wall you're leaning on until its gone. Then you find God. The result is being transformed into his likeness. Instead of just *giving* an offering, we *are* the offering. We are not our own; we belong completely to him.

Paul paints a picture of this total surrender by turning a familiar Old Testament picture on its head. Instead of a slain, burning animal literally going up in flames on the altar as an offering, Paul says we are to be a "living" sacrifice.[26] This is a picture of total devotion. In the desert, God tests us to see if we will live for him.

"There are things that God does in the desert that he could never do in the 'river.' If you take the desert out of the story of the Bible, you don't have a story. If we want to do life with God, we'll have to go to the desert."[27]

The temptations of Jesus

For forty days, Jesus ate no food. The devil said to him, "If you are the Son of God, tell this stone to become bread." Jesus answered, "It is written: 'Man shall not live on bread alone.'"[28] Jesus didn't want to go outside the boundaries the Father had set up for him—this was an appointed time of fasting. The devil tempted Jesus to look for provision and satisfaction outside of the boundaries set by his Father. Jesus passed the test by humbling himself to the Father's will. For Jesus, there was no selfish use of power. Because of his purity of purpose, there was no landing place for this temptation. Jesus already knew he was God's Son and he didn't have to prove it with miracles.

In all of these desert temptations, Jesus shows amazing restraint. For Jesus, there is nothing wrong with making bread from a stone, but only if it's done for the Father's glory and under his authority. Jesus refused to take any short cuts. He waited for the times and places of the Father's choosing.

This is incredibly important, especially for anyone in a leadership position. We must refuse to show off our gifts from a selfish motive. We must always follow Jesus' example of refusing to manipulate people through our own illicit use of power. We must eradicate "landing pads" for temptation by purifying our motives and strengthening our devotion to our Father.

Learn to lean on him

We all have different "walls" that we lean on in life. We are tempted to fill the empty spaces in our lives with many things. Leaders who are insecure and ambitious for notoriety will be susceptible to showing off their gifts. Others have an over-dependence of food or sex or money.

If you love to be on the stage of ministry, and God "takes away that wall" you're leaning on, maybe that's a good thing. Maybe he is weaning you of your dependence on the high you get from being in front of people.

Do I mean the "high" you feel isn't the anointing of the Holy Spirit? Probably not all of it is the Holy Spirit. It's probably a mix of human emotions, the power of music, and the Holy Spirit. After 43 years of leading worship, in certain worship leading situations I still can feel my flesh being tugged on by a lust for glory. The flesh is always with us. We must stay aware that the devil is always waiting for the opportune time to tempt us. Maybe your "high" is closing big sales deals on your job. There's nothing wrong with doing well at work unless it's consuming you and forcing you to compromise your faith.

We feel significant when we're successful. We might be doing ministry...or building skyscrapers or...you fill in the blank. There's nothing wrong with being successful in your occupation. But sometimes God changes the landscape of our lives, and he asks us to say "no" to past behavior patterns or even our occupation. Maybe your "high" is buying a new pair of shoes. But you're finding that the emotional high from a shopping spree wears off way too fast, and it's too expensive. Maybe you feel God nudging you to find a different way to satisfy your craving.

The second test
In Jesus' second test in the wilderness, the devil showed him all the kingdoms of the world and said to him, "If you worship me, it will all be yours." Jesus didn't waver when the devil offered him, "all the kingdoms of this world." Jesus didn't take the bait. He didn't grasp for power and fame. He had all he needed in his Father. This ancient bond of love between Father and Son continued as Jesus walked the earth.

The type of temptations Satan threw at Jesus were directly related to the specific ministry he would soon begin. Very soon after the desert temptation, Jesus began doing miracles—turning water to wine, healing the sick and feeding large crowds from a little boy's lunch. He used his power for the right things. Jesus didn't use miracle power for his own gain.

If you have a public ministry that puts you in front of groups of people, you can be sure that you'll be tempted to misuse your position for selfish glory. Never fear! If you are utterly devoted to pleasing the Lord, you have nothing to worry about. When you begin to step into illegal territory, something in your soul will feel uncomfortable. Your built-in sensitivity meter, calibrated by the Holy Spirit, will not resonate with self-exalting choices. If you are eager to please God, he will give you access to his thoughts.

We need love, not riches, power or fame
When we are rooted and grounded in the Father's love, we don't *need* to grasp for riches or notoriety. We don't need to parade our gifts to prove a point. When we know the Father's favor, we can stand against temptation. We have confidence that choosing his ways is best.

The "letting go" lesson begins when we become Christians. Along the way, God gives us an occasional refresher course in the desert. Suddenly we realize God is saying to us, "It's time for a new course called 'Letting Go 301.' It's required curriculum for this season of your life." We are transformed through a purifying journey into powerlessness and back. Like Jesus, we allow power to be taken from us. As John the Baptist said, "He must increase, but I must decrease."[29]

"Some form of suffering is necessary to teach us how to live beyond the illusion of control and to give that control back to God. God is somehow in our suffering, and can even use it for good. If you don't get that, you close up and close down."[30]

Living in Humility

The natural reaction of the ego is to protect itself. When life takes an unexpected turn, don't get bitter, get better. Empty yourself of trying to control things and you'll get filled with more of God. Everything in us wants to avoid suffering. But if God is the author of your desert journey, don't try to escape. Instead, find help from the Lord in the desert. In Paul's letter to the suffering church in Thessalonica, he doesn't pray for the suffering to stop. He prays for the believers' hearts to be strengthened and for their love for one another to increase and overflow.

if you're in the desert, ask God what he's doing in you. Keep your heart open. Don't let your ego win the battle for your heart. When you feel like you're out of control of your life, maybe God is inviting you into deeper friendship with him. These times help us learn faith, loyalty and endurance. We grow in our friendship with God regardless of what we are "getting out of the deal." A real friend sticks close when there are no special benefits or pay back. God treasures our trust and faith in him in the midst of our weakness.

Is there a "wall" you're leaning against that is outside of the Father's boundaries for you? Find contentment by letting go of false supports. Let go of your ideas and get God's ideas. Take the humble road. Let go of past patterns of behavior that hinder you. Don't lay claim to your position and privilege if it steals you away from God's best for you. If God is leading you to let go of something, just let go. You'll have more peace. You'll be happier. If you have a hugely demanding job that pays well but it is stealing you away from your family, maybe you need to make an adjustment.

Ask your Papa, "What's next?" He'll give you grace for the next step. True happiness comes from letting go of false supports and being a trusting child who is strongly attached to a loving Father God. Then you can get ready for the next step of your faith adventure.

4

The Humble are Hungry for Righteousness

All kinds of people were attracted to Jesus because of his love, authority and humility. A few of the elite of society were drawn to him...a Roman soldier who had huge faith in Jesus' healing power...a Pharisee named Nicodemus from the upper echelons of religious leadership. But mostly it was unremarkable, unreligious and poor people that liked to hang out with him.

Why were they drawn to him? Many reasons—they were hungry; Jesus could multiply food. They were sick; Jesus was a healer. Many were simply awed by his miracles and they recognized the remarkable authority in his teaching—they knew the source of his authority was from higher up. His appearance in Judea was the biggest thing they had ever seen.

People flocked to the humble King because he was open-hearted and welcoming. "Come to me all who are weary and weighed down... I am gentle and humble in heart...come to me and find rest for your souls." They felt accepted by Jesus—and at the same time, challenged to seek the higher life. He didn't stand at a distance from the common folk with a condescending attitude. He was ready to engage in conversation with people of any nationality, religion, or gender. He must have been a good listener. He never looked down on people because they were different from him. He didn't discriminate against anyone. But he was sometimes hard on the Pharisees who didn't really love God and were hindering the common folk from knowing God.

People felt comfortable around him because he wasn't judging them. He was befriending them. For Jesus, there was no favoritism. No looking down his nose at the "undesirables" of society. To him they were all desirable. Judging by the reaction of the "sinners," who were his close friends, he was extremely approachable. He spoke a challenging message, but also a joyful one, full of hope. For his first public miracle, he changed around 150 gallons of water into wine for a wedding. He knew how to have a good time. His "coming out" miracle wasn't a healing or a sermon, it was a sign of the superabundant joy he would bring.

There was something magnetic about Jesus—He drew people to himself. Some people called him a prophet. A few called him the Messiah. Whatever label they gave him, they sensed righteousness. Some, like Zaccheus the tax collector, knew there was no choice but to follow Jesus. To get into the Jesus way of life, his closest disciples threw caution to the wind, let go of their past life and began their apprenticeship with Jesus.

Zaccheus, the tax collector who was hungry for righteousness
John Wimber often said, "The way in is the way on." The way *in* to the kingdom is by receiving God's grace, turning away from sin and towards Jesus. The way *on* in the kingdom is to continue doing exactly the same thing. It sounds crazy, but as sincere followers of Jesus, we can sometimes forget who Jesus actually *is*. We get caught up in the routines of life without focusing on the person, the heart and the example of Jesus. The story of Zaccheus reminds us that following Jesus means getting every obstacle out of the way of his righteousness in our lives. Following Jesus is much more than singing songs to him, giving money to the church and being nice to our family. It means getting rid of sinful habits by his grace.

The Humble Are Hungry for Righteousness

The story of Zaccheus[47] is a remarkable story of repentance and salvation. But the application of this story goes way beyond the conversion experience. Zac was transformed from a life of greed into being a follower of Jesus who generously repaid those he had wronged. Zac shows us how to keep going on in kingdom ways by practicing the pursuit of righteousness.

Zaccheus was a chief tax collector, an employee of the Roman empire. The Romans wanted to collect as much tax as they could without tying up their own personnel. They recruited locals, like Zaccheus, and gave them a percentage of what was collected. Anything these locals raised over the amount due to the government was their personal profit. Luke says Zaccheus was a wealthy man, so he must have extorted a great deal from the people and encouraged his subordinates to do so as well. In this time and culture, tax collectors were despised by the Jews. They weren't even allowed into the inner court of the temple to worship. They were treated as dirty outcasts.

When Jesus came to Jericho, Zac was *desperate* to see him. He had clearly undergone a drastic change of heart *before* Jesus came to town. Nothing was going to stop Zac from getting close to Jesus. His actions showed that he didn't care what *anyone* except Jesus thought of him. Zac's fascination with Jesus was much more than superficial curiosity about a famed miracle worker. Zac wanted to change his ways. He was ready to repent. This single-minded zeal of Zaccheus reminds us what it's like to have Jesus as our *first love*.

When Jesus showed up, a big crowd gathered to see him. Why was a crowd following Jesus? Because he had been healing people all over Judea! Throughout Galilee he was "proclaiming the good news of the kingdom, and healing every disease and sickness among the people."[48] He was hugely famous throughout the region. When Jesus came to town, the news spread like wildfire.

In his hometown of Jericho, Zac was infamous as a crooked tax collector. Zac and his cohorts had certainly shown up at the front door of many of the people in this crowd, demanding exorbitant tax fees. Zac knew that the Jews hated him. They considered him to be the dirtiest kind of sinner. Though he was a Jew, he was colluding with the despised Roman government. Zac's brothers saw him as a traitor.

Zac was a short guy; he couldn't see over the crowd. So he ran ahead and climbed a sycamore-fig tree. Climbing trees was for little boys—not a dignified thing to do for a wealthy man who had many employees. When Jesus saw Zac in the tree, he could see what was in Zac's heart. We see in many gospel stories, as with the Samaritan woman and the critical Pharisees, that Jesus knew the motives and thoughts of his hearers. In this case, Jesus could see Zac's genuine desire to turn from his life of greed and extortion. He could see Zac's hunger for righteousness.

Jesus saw past Zaccheus' crimes and into his heart, so he reached out a hand of friendship to Zac, saying, "Zaccheus, come down immediately. I must stay at your house today." Zac must have been blown away, thinking, "Why does he want to hang out with *me*?" In the Ancient Near East, to eat with someone was to call them your close friend. Jesus was making a statement in front of all these people, "Zac, I want you to be my friend." Inviting himself to the tax-collector's home was an offer of forgiveness, mercy, and acceptance. The onlookers knew this, and were stunned. They started grumbling, "This man is a notorious sinner! And Jesus is going home to eat with him." Everyone knew Zac was a crook.

To illustrate the weight of Zac's sin and the amazing grace of Jesus, here's a modern-day example. Do you remember the Enron scandal in 2001? Enron had become the largest seller of natural gas in North America by 1992. Through the 90's, the company started going downhill fast, but the executives covered it up through using accounting loopholes and poor financial reporting. To keep the investors and shareholders in the dark, they were dishonest about the income and debts of the company.

The Humble Are Hungry for Righteousness

Eventually, Enron went bankrupt. Enron's $63.4 billion in assets made it the largest corporate bankruptcy in U.S. history. Thousands of investors and employees of the company lost all their investments. Many executives at Enron were indicted for a variety of charges and some were later sentenced to prison. Kenneth Lay was the face of the Enron scandal, a top news story. Stories were told on major TV networks of 30-year employees with Enron who had lost all their retirement savings. You could see the terrible injustice for the employees who lost their jobs and all their money.

Imagine the disgust and hatred towards Kenneth Lay and the other Enron executives from the employees and investors who were deceived and bankrupted. This kind of disgust and loathing is what people felt towards Zaccheus, the tax collector. Now imagine seeing Kenneth Lay coming to the altar of a Billy Graham crusade after the collapse of Enron. Imagine he was truly repentant, and sorry for his sins. He was ready to receive and follow Jesus. How would Jesus have responded to Kenneth Lay? In the same way he responded to Zaccheus—warmly welcoming him as a friend.

This radical grace shown by Jesus is the *main reason* we are so attracted to him. It's what makes us want to be *like him*. Receiving God's grace makes us want to live in it and give it away.

A change of heart marked by outward action

After Jesus invited himself to Zac's house for lunch, Zac astonished the onlookers with this statement: "Look, Lord! Here and now I give *half of my possessions to the poor*, and if I have cheated anybody out of anything, I will pay back *four times* the amount." Whoa! When Jesus offered a hand of friendship, Zac promised to re-pay four times the stolen amount to anyone he has cheated! John Wimber used to say of Zaccheus' response, "If that's not salvation, it will do until salvation gets here!"

Jesus said of Zac's promise: "Today *salvation has come* to this house, because this man, too, is a son of Abraham." Zaccheus was a Jew, "a son of Abraham." He probably knew that the Jewish law required at the very least a full repayment of stolen goods, and in some cases, an extra 20%.[49] In other cases, a person had to pay back double what he had stolen.[50]

Zac went way over any requirement of Jewish law, offering to pay back quadruple the stolen amount. Zac's over-the-top generosity makes me think of the woman who lavished her tears and costly perfume on Jesus feet.[51] Jesus said of this woman who had lived a sinful life, "when you are forgiven much, you love much." So it was for Zaccheus. He sensed Jesus' lavish love and forgiveness and was moved to respond with generosity.

Notice that Jesus had not required anything of Zaccheus before offering friendship to him. Jesus, who knows all hearts, offered *grace to the humble* in this story. Zac had been forgiven much. He responded with overflowing generosity. When we encounter the extravagant grace of God, we want to do the same for others. We are cut to the depth of our heart and want nothing else but to please the Lord.

Zaccheus committed not only to a change of *belief*, but a change of *behavior*—from greed and dishonesty to generosity and justice. Notice that he did not buy his forgiveness through this gift to the poor. Mercy was offered to him by Jesus *before* Zac promised to make things right. Zac intuitively sensed the mercy being offered to him and responded in like kind—with an extravagant promise of generosity.

Inner and outer purity
I wonder if Zaccheus was on the mountainside listening to Jesus give the Sermon on the Mount. I wonder if he heard Jesus say, "your righteousness must *exceed* that of the Pharisees." I wonder if he heard Jesus confront the Pharisees who "cleaned the outside of the cup" but not the inside. They neglected the root issues of love, purity and righteousness. It seems to me that Zac had caught the idea that outward actions aren't the only important thing. It's the motives and the heart behind your actions. Zac was seeking inner purity along with outward righteous acts.

The Humble Are Hungry for Righteousness

Zaccheus had abused his powerful position as a tax collector. This is just the kind of thing Jesus confronted in the Sermon on the mount. Jesus' words cut to the core of abusive relationships. He called people to lay down their power and learn what real love is. He said, "The problem is not just the issue of murder. It's the *anger* and *hatred* that underlies murder. "...anyone who is *angry* with a brother or sister will be subject to judgment...go and be reconciled to them." So, get rid of your hatred.

Imagine the people who saw that first meeting between Jesus and Zaccheus. Some of those who had been cheated by Zac would later come to him, livid with anger, yelling at him for his thieving ways. Some may have threatened him. Situations like this are the moment of decision for both sides of an argument.

Would Zac's victims remember Jesus' teaching to seek peace and reconciliation instead of retribution? Would Zac remember Jesus' teaching to turn the other cheek? Jesus taught us to make ourselves vulnerable to those who mistreat us instead of retaliating. In the ancient Near East, the law of retaliation was widely accepted. It was legal to pursue vengeance or retaliation. You could take something of equal value from someone to replace what they took from you. Jesus tells us not to insist on being paid back. Instead, be willing to suffer being wronged. Lay down your power.

Jesus also said, "If anyone slaps you on the right cheek, turn to them the other cheek also."[52] Hitting someone on the right cheek was a form of public disgrace. It was done with a backhand hit using the right hand to the right cheek. Jesus says "turn the other cheek." Then, the left cheek is exposed, opening yourself to a violent strike with right hand to left cheek. So, you're making yourself vulnerable.[53]

That day in front of a big crowd, Zaccheus made himself vulnerable. By exposing himself as a sinner, he invited his victims to come to him. In his first conversation with Jesus, he made the right choice and it was a tough choice. What we don't know is what he did later. Did he follow through

Living in Humility

with his public promise? So far, I've treated this story as if Zac completely made good on his promise to repay the stolen tax money. But we don't really know if he actually repaid the money. Right motivation must be followed up with right action. For Jesus, integrity meant inner and outer righteousness.

Let's revisit the core meaning of humility for a moment. It means to bow to God's wishes. It means to be poor in spirit, which means allowing God's ways to win the day. With that in mind, is there any area of your life where your actions aren't lining up with your desires to do right? Is there any restitution you need to make to someone? We have to be careful not to revel in our interior knowledge of God's love while neglecting outward action—*doing* what is right.

Jesus urges us to build bridges of relationship with others by being willing to suffer wrong. He taught us to give generously to those in need, and to do it in secret, not for the purpose of gaining a reputation. (I believe Zaccheus' public promise to repay stolen money and give to the poor was an exception to this teaching of Jesus to "give in secret." Since Zac was widely known as an agent of the Roman government who routinely cheated people, a public statement of repentance and a promise to make restitution was appropriate.)

This kind of righteousness requires a changed heart. We can't just conform to religious rules. If we immerse ourselves in God's gracious love, we'll be empowered to repent and overcome our anger, lust, and greed. God gives grace (strength to do what is right) to the humble. His Spirit, joined to our own spirit, empowers us to do right.

Jesus said to Thomas, "if you've seen me, you've seen the Father."[54] When we see Jesus gladly welcoming a hated tax collector like Zac, we get a picture of the Father's gracious love and mercy towards us. His kindness makes it easy for us to turn to him. His empowering grace makes it possible to obey.

This is the mark of a humble response to Jesus—you will uproot the darkness in your own heart and follow through by doing right. Humility leads to repentance from our deeds of darkness and the root issues of those actions.

Humility: doing the right thing
Those who witnessed Jesus' earthly life saw a leader standing up for righteousness. They saw injustice being overturned. They saw in Jesus a powerful person making a priority of helping the weak and rejected. They were attracted to his grace and righteousness. We admire those who do the right thing, and we want to be like them. We know in our gut that it's the right thing to do.

God puts a sense of right and wrong into the consciousness of all his children. There are plenty of non-Christian people in the world who "act justly and show mercy."[55] That's because they're made in God's image. And they know in their gut that righteousness is right. When they see someone doing justice and showing mercy, it rings true in their hearts.

Here is Jesus' humility: his mission was to help people, regardless of the cost. He didn't care about being rejected by the religious authorities. He did what was important, not what was convenient. He was well liked by many people, but his popularity was never what motivated him. He wasn't about pleasing people. Everyone loved Jesus for his forgiveness, his healings, his feeding the poor, and his raising the dead. But not everyone could accept Jesus' radical call to a changed heart and self-sacrificial love.

When Zaccheus left his tax collecting business, he had to change both his outward habits and his heart. He had to stop extorting money from people for his own gain. He had to make himself vulnerable to being mistreated. And those who came to Zac for repayment had to learn to love a man who used to be their bitter enemy.

Just like Zaccheus, we must build bridges of relationship. We must use our power for good, not to take advantage of people. We must get rid of our anger and pursue reconciliation and repent from lust and pursue purity. We should do our good works in secret, not to gain a reputation. We should "go the extra mile" and do *more* than we are asked when someone needs help.

Follow Zac's example of childlike zeal. Let nothing stop you from seeing Jesus—climb a tree if you have to. Do what he asks of you. Cast aside your fears of any critical onlookers.

Every time we catch ourselves thinking, desiring or acting unrighteously, we must turn away from sin and towards Jesus to receive his grace. God helps the humble. You can go far in your faith by praying the prayer of the tax collector, "Lord, have mercy on me, a sinner." Praying that prayer opens the windows of heaven—God's enabling power for you to do what is right. Remember, Jesus will respond to you the same way he did to Zaccheus, "I want to be your friend."

Like Zaccheus, we've been drawn to Jesus because of his incomparable love. We find comfort from the one who described himself as "lowly and humble of heart." Having received that comfort, may we never be numb to Jesus' teachings of doing right. Humility means doing things the Jesus way. As we practice these things, we are formed into Christlikeness.

5

A Teenage Girl Says Yes to God

Pretend for a moment that you are the main character in this unimaginable situation. You are a 13-year old girl, engaged to be married. A huge angel shows up to announce that you're going to get pregnant by the Holy Spirit. This gigantic shining angelic being is staring you in the face and you feel overwhelmed.

Yes, you know the story. Put yourself in Mary's shoes for a moment. "The angel greeted Mary and said, "You are truly blessed! The Lord is with you."[56] This is the angel Gabriel we're talking about. When Gabriel appeared to Daniel around 600 years before Christ, Daniel was so terrified, he fell facedown on the ground. He was sick for days after his experience with the angel.[57] Aside from being very afraid, what were Mary's thoughts? "OK, what do you want from me? I've never seen an angel before and I'm scared."

The frightening angel continues, "Mary, you have nothing to fear. God has a surprise for you: You will become pregnant and give birth to a son and call his name Jesus. He will be great, be called 'Son of the Highest.'[58] God "has a surprise" for Mary—that was the understatement of the century.

Living in Humility

There are different kinds of surprises in life. Like, "your house just burned down!" or your boss says, "I'm sorry but this is your last day." I wonder if in the first few moments of this encounter with the angel, Mary saw Gabriel's visit as a *bad* surprise. We don't know what she thought.

Perhaps Mary was thinking, "What this angel just told me has nothing to do with what my mother taught me about pregnancy!" No woman in history had ever become "pregnant by the Holy Spirit." Did Mary say to herself, "Do I really have a choice in the matter?" There's no way we can know exactly what she though or felt. But you have to wonder...

Mary was a regular teenage girl
When we hear this story at Christmas time, we frame it kind of like a fairy tale. Because we know the end of the story, we think, "of course, Mary did the right thing." We say, "O yeah, the virgin birth, how amazing!" But this miracle was completely unprecedented. Maybe Mary wondered, "are you a *good* angel or...?" We can't possibly understand or experience the shock and angst this teenager felt.

Mary said to the angel, "How could I get pregnant if I've never slept with a man?"[59] When the angel explained she would conceive a child by the Holy Spirit, I wonder if it made her feel any better. Mary was a typical young teenager in ancient Israel. She probably spent very little time outside of her own home and neighborhood. It was customary that women weren't allowed to talk to men unless their father was present.

In first century Palestine, women were seen as second class citizens. (Jesus would soon be turning that tradition upside down.) In Mary's time, women simply did what men in authority told them to do. "Well behaved" women really didn't have a choice—do what the man tells you to do, or in this case, do what the giant man-angel tells you.

Whatever her first reactions were, by the end of the conversation with this male angel, she said, "OK, let God's will be done with me." She was convinced that this messenger was truly from God. She must have been thinking, "I don't know exactly what I'm getting myself into, but here I go. My gut tells me this is right."

Isn't that what hearing from God is like? This is how Peter and John just *knew* it was right when Jesus said to them, "come, follow me." There's no other explanation for why they *immediately* left their jobs to follow Jesus, the preacher-healer. It's the same reason that Matthew left his job *immediately* when Jesus invited him to "come, follow me."

Mary's heart was tuned to God
I think the best explanation for Mary's response to the angel is that she was already a devout God-follower. Mary was doing her best to love and follow Yahweh. God knows all things; he chose Mary for this unique once-in-history assignment. God knew she had a heart that was ready to respond to him. That doesn't mean God forced her to say 'yes.' He waited for her response. "I am the Lord's servant," Mary answered. "May your word to me be fulfilled."[60] Somehow, despite the craziness of God's call on her life, she knew it was right.

Something about the angel's words rang true because she had already developed a sensitivity to the Spirit of God, a humility that predisposed her to agree with whatever God said to her.

"I didn't ask for this"
Mary's visit from the angel Gabriel was over-the-top dramatic—like something out of a Hollywood movie. There were roughly nine months for Mary to ponder the words of the angel while she felt the baby grow inside her.

Then, things got tough. Mary and her betrothed Joseph had to endure rejection and accusations of Mary carrying an illegitimate child. Then they had to leave town because of a warning that Herod was ordering all newborn boys to be killed. News of a coming King had leaked out.

Living in Humility

I wonder if Mary asked God, "Why did you have to choose *me* to do this?" Being the mother of Jesus was not a job Mary chose. God chose. This young teenager had no idea of the agony and ecstasy awaiting her in this role.

Some of us had the option of choosing an occupation. For others, it feels like our job was thrust upon us. We took the best opportunity we could find. Or we took the *only* thing available. Maybe you are working in your family's business and you often think, "I didn't ask for this." It might be a roller coaster experience, or it might be a boring job that has nothing to do with your real passions in life.

God's calling

One of the most frequent descriptions of God's people in the New Testament is being "called" by God. Paul was *called* to be an apostle. Every Christian is "*called* to belong to Jesus Christ." All Christians are "loved by God and *called* to be saints," and are "*called* according to his purpose." We are all called to belong to his family, receive his love and represent God in our daily lives. Our calling determines how we live, think and act.

How do *God's calling* and life's *coincidences* collide? How do you feel about your current job or occupation? Are you a mother, (in other words, someone who works around the clock with few breaks), or do you work in a business office or are you a teacher or truck driver? How do you view your occupation? Do you believe it's something God gave you? You might not enjoy what you're doing everyday. Like many people called to very difficult occupations, you might be saying, "I didn't ask for this."

I know a lot of people who earned a 4-year college degree and couldn't find a job in their chosen field after graduation. They do the best they can, using their skills and experience, and they take what is available. If they don't like their job, does that mean they're not called by God to do it? No. It just means it's not what they expected would happen.

"Any kind of authentic calling usually takes us to a place where we have serious objections of some sort, places where we feel inadequate—where we confront our own willfulness and our own preconceived ideas about how we thought our life would go, where what we think God is asking us to do is downright impossible or where we just don't want to take the risk."[61]

A prisoner of Jesus
When the apostle Paul appealed to Caesar, and was taken to Rome and imprisoned, he didn't complain. He saw it as part of his calling. He introduced himself in his letter to the church in Philippi as, "Paul, a prisoner of Christ Jesus." Wow! He didn't say, "Paul, a prisoner of the Roman government." He saw God as sovereign over every situation.

Paul was so convinced of God's all-knowing, loving care for him, that he didn't hesitate to say he was a prisoner *of Jesus*. Paul saw Jesus as being *behind* the whole event. Did Paul begrudge this assignment from God? No, far from it!

Later in this letter, Paul is exhorting his friends in Philippi to "rejoice at all times!" Paul is the one in prison, and he's telling his friends to cheer up! Paul finds a way, by the grace of God, to be cheerful while chained to a bunch of prison guards. Indwelt by the Holy Spirit, we can conquer all kinds of annoying situations. Sometimes I complain if I'm "imprisoned" in a traffic jam that causes a 15-minute delay in my journey. I could use a good dose of increased faith in God's sovereignty!

Paul keeps company with the likes of Moses, Joseph and a host of other priests and prophets who did jobs they didn't ask for and didn't want. In Paul's case, we see the wisdom of God play out quickly in his prison assignment. Paul was chained to a series of Roman guards, most likely in 4-hour shifts throughout each day. Each of these guards was held captive to Paul's preaching of the gospel! Historical accounts from this time period tell us that members of the ruling family in the Roman government came to

Living in Humility

faith in Christ. There is a good chance that the elite guardsmen who were with Paul passed the good news on to royal family members.

What about single mothers who have been deserted by their husband or boyfriend? There are certainly hundreds of thousands of these in the world at this moment, if not millions. The world is unfortunately full of irresponsible men who sire several children and then desert their wife. With no husband to provide income, and a 24-7 role of mothering a baby, a single mother can feel trapped in a prison of loneliness and poverty.

Humility is required when we feel like we're in some kind of prison. A thousand times we must say, "God, this is your thing. You are in control. I can't control my life. I can't control my boss. I can't control my students...my children's behavior...my clients. I can't control what kind of tasks are given to me. But as long as I'm in this position I will serve you and the people around me."

Working a "normal job" is as much a calling from God as the priest's work. Whatever your station in life may be—wife, husband, son or daughter—these are all "callings" from God. There is no divide between secular and sacred. We do it *all to the Lord*.

Early in her mothering life, my wife read a book written by a Benedictine Monk, Dom Humbert van Zeller. The book is, "Holiness for Housewives: and Other Working Women."[62] Linda wondered what this unmarried man could know about being a housewife or mother? But his message had a lasting impact. Basically, the author wrote that if you find yourself having and raising children, *that is part of your calling from God*. Period, full stop. You accept the job that falls in your lap as a divine calling, even if you didn't plan or expect it.

It's a trust issue. Some people come from a family of lawyers, or real estate sales or teachers. So, they naturally follow that path. We all have a certain background and a unique road to walk. Can you trust that God is fair and just even if you didn't come from a well educated family who could give you all the best training and modeling as a child and teenager?

Here we see the intersection of faith and humility. "Yes, God, I accept the way you made me, and all the thousands of events and personal traits I have that have brought me to the place I am today."

I sometimes wish I was a businessman. I admire people who are strong Christians and are also successful in business. Recently, I heard a talk from one such businessman. He was encouraging a group of his peers to be generous in donating to a very fruitful ministry that he really believed in. During his talk, as I was admiring his heart and his journey in life, God said to me, "you are an arrow."

In other words, God was saying, "I didn't call you into business. You're an arrow that I like to shoot anywhere I please to bring worship and the blessings of my kingdom." For me, it means going to serve at home and to write songs and books, and to go to various countries in the world to share what I have.

You do the job no matter how you feel
Walking out your calling in life is about humbling yourself to a God-given occupation. If you're a parent, your job is to nurture and train little people who will grow up to be influencers of others. You will impact them more deeply than any one else on the planet. If you don't have children, you still influence thousands of people in your life by your character, your words and what you do with your time and energy.

In her years of raising Jesus (sounds funny) I wonder how many times Mary found herself daydreaming about being a "normal mother." Mary suffered many traumatic experiences being the Messiah's mother. There had to be benefits too, like waking up in the morning to find that your sick sheep were mysteriously brought back to full health overnight. Or the

Living in Humility

time when a broken table leg suddenly was as good as new. When the wine ran out at a wedding, Mary knew who could take care of the problem.

But when Jesus started his public ministry, everything went topsy-turvy. Think of the talk around Mary's family table: "Jesus has lost his mind. Who does he think he is?" And when they realized he was healing people all over the place, and feeding thousands of hungry people, Mary had to face another demanding challenge. Think of all the talk in the neighborhood, "Look what your son is doing!" "Can your boy come to *my house* to turn the water to wine?"

I've had a few experiences of neighbors saying, "Look what your son is doing!" But those were *not* happy moments or happy neighbors! My sons were not healing and feeding people! They were doing things like lighting fires and hurling grapefruits into neighbors swimming pools and puncturing bicycle tires and…I could tell you many more stories. (To be fair, my kids also did lots of good and helpful things).

If you have children, you know that parenting can be very demanding and upsetting. In your moments of weakness you may ask yourself, "when is this going to end?" In case I didn't already mention it, I have eight children. I have no regrets about having a large family, just occasional feelings of being overwhelmed.

There are plenty of overwhelming tasks aside from parenthood that God uses to shape us into his image. How about serving people as an airlines agent, a food server or a traffic cop? How about caring for addicts? Or caring for your aging, ailing parents? Or working in a home for disabled people? Or teaching a first-grade class in a low income neighborhood? You may think your occupation isn't very important. God sees a different reality!

If you feel like "I didn't really ask for this job," you've joined the ranks of Mary, Moses, Joseph and scores of others who end up on a path they never could have predicted. They all chose to let God spend them however he wanted. Mary got the surprise of her life when Gabriel showed up. But she chose to say, "I am the Lord's servant. Let your will be done."

We can't predict our future

Having a large family wasn't something my wife imagined early in life. Her goal in her late teens was to become a single missionary. Marriage wasn't interesting to her. That all changed, and after we were married for five years, she caught a vision to have children, and the rest is history. We ran with that vision. And we're still running! We enthusiastically jumped into having kids. We treasure our family. But we've paid a big price on many levels, just as all parents do.

Parenting is one long haul *calling* from God that requires a lot of patience, perseverance and humility. Yikes, the things your pre-teens and teenagers will say to you. On many days, you will think, "the grass is greener on the other side of the fence."

Maybe your long haul calling isn't parenting, but staying in the same job or occupation you've had for 25-plus years. As you humble yourself to your calling, like Mary did, God forms you into a loyal, trustworthy, unselfish person. Remind yourself that you *are called* by God to be an ambassador of his love and peace, wherever you may find yourself.

All of us have an opportunity to leave a legacy that will outlast our own lives, no matter what our occupation is. Mary counted it a great honor to carry the Christ child and nurture his early life. May we all recognize the great privilege of loving the people God puts around us, even if it feels sometimes as if we're imprisoned.

Here is an excerpt from the song Mary sang after her visitation from the angel Gabriel: "My soul glorifies the Lord and my spirit rejoices in God my Savior, for he has been mindful of the humble state of his servant."[63]

Living in Humility

Change in God's pocket

Rich Nathan, pastor of the Vineyard Church in Columbus, Ohio, shared in a sermon, "John Wimber used to say that we need to be loose change in the pocket of the Lord that he can spend any way he sees fit. If you want to spend me right where I am, spend me, Lord. If you want to spend me overseas, spend me there, dear God. If you want to spend me in this ministry or this job or this non-profit or working with kids or elderly people or whatever, do so." Have you ever said, "God, I give you the absolute right in this season of my life." You may be a young person and single or you may be a retiree or an empty nester."[64]

I heard John use this term "change in God's pocket" many times in sermons. It's a picture that sticks with me. In our culture, people feel entitled to all kinds of privileges. In God's great plan, he can do with us whatever he wants to.

"Come to Latin America"

Earlier this year I was in Mazatlan, Mexico, teaching and leading worship at a Vineyard church that reaches out to many groups of poor people in the greater Mazatlan area. One of the last nights, I was leading worship in a training meeting for local Mexican church members.

The meeting wasn't well attended. I have to admit it's hard to fly thousands of miles to a place, and sometimes only a small group of people show up to the meetings. But it's worth it (*vale le pena*). It's all about partnering with local churches who are pouring out their lives to reach needy people.

Though the meeting was small, on this occasion I was really enjoying leading worship in Spanish. When the worship set was finished, I turned away from the microphone to walk offstage and I spontaneously started singing, "I'm change in your pocket, you can spend me however you want to." Since that time, I've developed the little tune that began in that moment into a complete song.

On another trip to Latin America this year, God spoke to me clearly, reaffirming a previous word. I was leading worship and teaching at a Vineyard church in Santiago, Chile. After the meeting, I sat down on the front row and the Holy Spirit came on me powerfully, so I sat quietly and waited. God said to me very clearly, two times: "Keep coming to Latin America."

This was part of God's answer to a prayer I frequently pray: "God, what do you want me to do next?" Just to be clear, there's nothing more spiritual about going to a different continent than there is in helping people in our own neighborhoods. It just happens to be part of what I do. What has he called you to do?

I love Madeleine L'Engle's description of humility: "Humility is throwing oneself away in complete concentration on something or someone else." [65] This is an apt description of Jesus' life on earth. He threw himself away for our sake, in obedience to his Father. But all along, he knew the end of the story. He knew he would be re-united with his Father and reign with him.

May we anticipate good things from God as we say "yes" to his calling on our lives.

6

Doing, Seeing and Being Jesus

"I believe the greatest joy one can have is doing something for someone else without any thought of getting something in return."[66] *John Wooden, former UCLA basketball coach*

Jesus did the dirty work
One of the great highlights of Jesus' servant life was his washing of the disciples' feet. This was a task reserved for the household servants. The grime and stench of this task was nasty. The dirt roads in Jesus' day were filled with animal droppings and all kinds of filth. Peter was shocked when Jesus asked to serve him in this way. He forcefully resisted Jesus' offer.

Since we don't have muddy streets to walk through, what would a modern day equivalent of foot washing be? In his classic book, *The Jesus Style,* Gayle D. Erwin shares some examples of modern-day foot washing:

"When someone takes the time to listen to me, I feel as if my feet have been washed. When I am complimented, my feet have been washed. When someone shares a joy with me, my feet have been washed. When someone values my ear enough to share a burden or confess, my feet have been washed."[67]

A Lifetime of Loyalty

From a distance, I watched my father care for my diseased mother for the last seven years of her life. They were in Los Angeles and I live in greater Vancouver, Canada. She suffered from Alzheimer's disease and many physical problems. In his mid-70s and early 80s, my Dad was her primary care giver. Because he had a serious heart condition, giving 24/7 care was very strenuous.

Finally, in the last two years of her life, we had no choice but to move my mother into a fulltime care facility. Her mind and body had deteriorated so much that it was impossible to keep her at home. Because I lived so far away, I couldn't offer much help. I visited Los Angeles several times a year and always visited my Mom in the care home each day I was in town. My two sisters and my father lived locally and bore the brunt of the load of caring for Mom.

Because of her illness, in those last years she was often cranky and demanding. This was such a contrast to her former lighthearted, fun-loving personality. For most of her life, she had an unforgettable laugh that would rise above the noise in a crowded room. During her long, slow decline in health, she became an entirely different person. Even while she was still alive, we were grieving the loss of the mother we had known and loved our whole lives.

Serving those who can't return the favor

A mentally ill person is unable to have a normal conversation much less express appreciation to a loving caregiver. Serving someone who can't return the love isn't easy, but it forms us into more loving people. We do our best to love unselfishly, moment- by-moment, day by day. But we're frustrated because we can't understand why God allows a person to suffer for so long.

Visiting my Mom was a type of modern-day foot washing. I remember the ache in my stomach as I arrived and parked on the street in front of her care home. It was agonizing to see her so confused and helpless. Often, her first words to me were, "What are you doing here?" I would lift her into her wheelchair and take her to the patio to feed her and chat with her. Conversation was difficult.

We learn humility in those situations. We often feel helpless. We're not in control of the process or the person. It's a simple act of kindness done in secret. It's a go-into-your-closet act of kindness.

We have no choice but to let go of the right to be respected or appreciated. We take the low, small place. We feel helpless because we can't fix our loved one. We can't make this fragile person whole. We know that only God can bring a change, so we wait, and wait some more, hanging onto hope. Sometimes we know we're not waiting for a healing, we're waiting for our family member to die. It's obvious that the end is near.

My respect for my father grew enormously as I watched him care compassionately for his wife during these trying years. He was fulfilling his wedding vows "to love and cherish her until death do us part." He was very frustrated at times but he kept on caring for her.

Here's one way to summarize what's important in life: care for *just one person* at a time. Heidi Baker, missionary to Africa, said: "I believe that Jesus would have given His life for just one person. Jesus emptied Himself, He humbled Himself and He so yielded Himself to His Father's love that He had no ambition of His own. He was not looking to build an empire, He did not want praise or adulation or to impress people with who or how many followed Him. He stopped over and over again for just one person, for just one life."[68]

Loneliness

I found out from the nursing staff in my mother's care home that many of the patients *never* received a visit from their relatives. Living there was a rough ordeal for my mother even with daily visits from her husband and

Living in Humility

children. I can't imagine how hard it would be to receive *no visits at all* from a loved one.

We live in a world filled with lonely and isolated souls. People are thirsty for real relationship. Visiting a hospitalized friend is an oasis of love for them. We patiently wait for them to find words to tell their story. In listening, we are generously giving of ourselves and take the humble place.

"According to a major study by a leading scholar of the subject, roughly 20 percent of Americans—about 60 million people—are unhappy with their lives because of loneliness. Across the Western world, physicians and nurses have begun to speak openly of an epidemic of loneliness...We are living in an isolation that would have been unimaginable to our ancestors...We have never been more detached from one another, or lonelier..."[69]

Mother Teresa hit the nail on the head when she said, "If you want to change the world, go home and love your family."[70] The world is changed one conversation at a time.

A life-changing conversation between mother and son

When he was 10 years old, David Eisenhower was vey excited about joining his older brothers to go trick-or-treating on Halloween night. But his parents wouldn't let him go. They thought he was too young. David threw a terrible temper tantrum. He begged his parents for the chance to join his brothers. In a rage, he screamed and cried and beat his hands against a tree.

His father spanked him and sent him to bed. Later on, his mother came to comfort her son, taking him into her lap and gently rocking him. After a time of quiet, she quoted Proverbs 16:32: "He that conquers his own soul is greater than he who takes a city." She explained to him how dangerous it was to hold bitterness in your heart towards others. Hanging onto anger will damage and imprison you.

Sixty-six years later, when he was seventy-six, Eisenhower wrote, "I have always looked back on that conversation as *one of the most valuable moments of my life.* To my youthful mind, it seemed to me that she talked for hours, but I suppose the affair was ended in fifteen or twenty minutes. At least she got me to acknowledge that I was wrong and I felt enough ease in my mind to fall off to sleep."[71]

Here is another example of foot-washing. In this case, we see the long lasting impact of sitting quietly with a person and speaking kind words. Ida Eisenhower was doing what all faithful mothers do. She was consoling and counseling her young boy. She couldn't have known she was shaping the character of a boy who would become President of the United States. She couldn't have known that this 20-minute conversation would always be remembered by her son as one of his most life-changing moments. The slow, steady, humble work of showing compassion to a weeping child has long-term benefits that we can't see in the moment of crisis. This was another "secret place" moment of showing love to a hurting child. God sees every kind word, every minute and hour you've spent in compassionate caring. God sees that kind of faithfulness and rewards it—even if it takes a long time. Through the centuries, mothers have had huge influence in shaping the character of their children and students, some of whom become leaders and influencers. Abraham Lincoln said, "All that I am, or hope to be, I owe to my angel mother."

What if David Eisenhower had turned out to have an unproductive, unremarkable life? What if he had spurned all of Ida's wisdom and guidance? Would that have changed the value of Ida's tender care for him? No. If you've loved, you've succeeded. If you "make love your highest goal," as the Apostle Paul says, you've done well. We can't control how the recipients of our love will respond.

Being and Seeing Jesus
Here is one more story illustrating the heart of humble service. Greg Paul began his foray into one of the poorest parts of Toronto in the early

Living in Humility

1990's. He volunteered with the AIDS Committee of Toronto (ACT) to help people with various household tasks. Later he pastored a church in a neighborhood filled with addicts, prostitutes and the homeless.

ACT assigned Greg to help a disabled man named Neil. His time with Neil was mundane for the first months but ended with a remarkable experience of God's revelation. Greg spent a winter shoveling Neil's walk, taking out the garbage, doing some grocery shopping and other chores. Because Neil was well off and could have easily afforded to pay for these services, Greg became irritated. Neil was good at accessing the various kinds of free support available to the disabled.

Despite wondering about the rightness of all this free help, Greg continued to serve Neil. After months of helping Neil, he realized that although Neil's practical needs were met, he was terribly isolated. Neil had no meaningful relationships with any of the various service providers who visited him. The helpers were all professional but relationally detached. Greg sensed that Neil wanted something besides practical help. He said, "I know I'm just supposed to help you out with odd jobs, but something tells me you'd rather have a friend. If that's what you want, I'd rather be a friend." Neil answered immediately, "I'd like that very much."[72]

Neil had a Mormon background and had created his own boutique spirituality with a potpourri of different philosophical ideas. All through their relationship, Greg waited patiently for the right moment to share Jesus with Neil. He didn't push the gospel story on Neil. He just served and waited until the right time. Greg continued to help Neil around the house, but they spent most of their time sitting and talking. They went on some excursions around town—to an art gallery, a park and an arboretum.

Around a year into this friendship, Neil's health began to deteriorate severely. Around Christmastime, Neil was confined to a wheelchair and dependent on an oxygen tank. He became disoriented, frightened and horribly emaciated. A few weeks later, Greg stopped in at Neil's place. He let himself into the house as usual and didn't find Neil downstairs. He climbed up the stairs to Neil's bedroom.

Greg writes, "Neil was writhing in a soundless panic in the bed, half sitting up, his pajama bottoms and the bed sheets wound around his ankles, his spindly arms flailing in a futile effort to free himself, a look of sheer terror on his face. He had soiled himself, and it was everywhere. He was disoriented, uncertain where he was or what was happening to him."[73] Greg ran a hot bath and carried Neil to the bathroom. He cleaned up the bed. After his bath, Greg carried Neil's frail body back to bed. Neil was mostly skin and bones, exhausted, and his skin was gray. Then Neil noticed that one of Greg's feet was still dirty, even after the bath.

"Getting a washcloth, I wiped that foot. As I did so, I was struck by what I can only describe as a powerful revelation, two streams of thought converging, and both seeming to me to be the voice of God. Cradling his foot in my hands, my mind was filled with the image of Jesus washing the feet of his disciples at the Last Supper, a towel around his waist, determinedly taking the servants role."[74] These words of Jesus pierced Greg's heart, "I needed clothes, and you clothed me, I was sick and you looked after me…. Whatever you did for one of the least of these brothers and sisters of mine, you did for me."

For more than a year, Greg had patiently waited to share Jesus with Neil. At this moment of vulnerability, Neil knew he was dying. He accepted Greg's offer of prayer. During the prayer, it seemed that Neil had drifted off to sleep, but then he finished Greg's prayer with a strong voice, "in the name of Jesus." By serving Neil, Greg made himself vulnerable. He let go of his power, stopped focusing on his own needs, and became present to a suffering person. God unveiled priceless truths to Greg as he laid down his life for a dying man. This friendship was based on unconditional love. Greg didn't require any "pay back" from Neil. His compassionate caring for Neil was done regardless of Neil's spiritual beliefs or sexual orientation.

Living in Humility

Greg reflects on how this experience shaped him. "I, who can heal no one, am reminded that being in his presence does not mean fixing everything. Being among people means being in their midst, not outside. It means being with them, not being over them. It means not looking away from their agony or humiliation, but beholding it, and having the courage to be also wounded by their pain."[75]

From this experience with Neil, Greg talks about "being and seeing Jesus." Not all of us have an epiphany like Greg did—a gift of spiritual sight by which we literally *see* Jesus in the person we are serving. For many of us, it's a more subtle realization of Jesus' words, "whatever you did for one of the least of these brothers and sisters of mine, you did for me."

By serving Neil, Greg very intentionally took a humble course of action. He submitted himself to the spiritual discipline of service. "A discipline is what is required of disciples: a deliberate choice, or series of choices, to follow and emulate the Master... In the spiritual life, discipline means to create that space in which something can happen that you hadn't planned or counted on. Being Jesus is a discipline of action."[76]

What do these three stories have in common?
Caring for one person at a time. Spending time doing simple, menial tasks with a hurting person. Sometimes, we just listen. Attending to another's needs when they can't help themselves. Receiving God's grace to perform difficult tasks and be with difficult people.

This is following Jesus' humble example of placing the needs of others above our own. Giving to someone who can't repay us. Making ourselves vulnerable like Jesus did. Being willing to not be in control of a situation—serving despite not being able to "fix" someone's problems. Loving someone regardless of how they respond to your love. Trusting God to be present and trusting him when he chooses to remain hidden.

7

Three Lives Poured Out

In following our humble King, we enter a life of service. Like Jesus, we will not always be appreciated by the people we help. In my view, Jesus seems to be one of the most unjustly treated persons in history. Though perfect, he was mistreated and punished. He told us, "The servant is not above his master." When we are mistreated, how will we respond?

In this chapter we take a look at three outstanding examples from the 17th and 20th centuries. They all show us that devotion to the Lord is the basis for our service to people. We may have to endure all kinds of injustice along the way. At the very least, we will have to do difficult jobs and work with ornery people. We learn from those who have gone before us that we don't need constant positive reinforcement to keep moving forward in our vocation. The Lord will sustain if all we do is an act of worship to him.

Frances Perkins
"When a person gives a poor man shoes, does he do it for the poor man or for God?" This was one of the questions Frances Perkins had to answer in her long journey of fighting for the rights of the poor—as a street-level worker, a workers-rights advocate and finally as a cabinet member in Franklin Roosevelt's White House.[77]

Living in Humility

In the year 1911, Perkins witnessed a horrible fire that killed 146 laborers in a clothing factory. Most of the victims were young women. The workers couldn't escape because the company hadn't complied with building safety regulations. Because of greed and disregard for the poor, the business owners hadn't implemented the safety measures required by law. There was outrage in the community for such horrible negligence.

This event was a huge catalyst in Perkins discovering her calling to a vocation of speaking up for those who couldn't defend themselves. She came from a privileged background with a good education, but she didn't follow the typical career path. Instead, she jumped into the rough world of fighting for reform. She was committed to the cause of helping marginalized people.

Eventually, Frances Perkins became the U.S. Secretary of Labor under President Franklin Roosevelt. She worked to secure unemployment benefits for laborers, pensions for elderly Americans, and welfare for the poorest Americans. She also helped craft laws against child labor.

Early on, she was a street-level worker with the hungry and homeless. It was hard work, and sometimes thankless. Perkins said, "The poor will often be ungrateful, and you will lose heart if you rely on immediate emotional rewards for your work. But if you do it for God, you will never grow discouraged."[78] This so important for all of us! In all we do, it is the Lord we serve.

One of Perkins' early jobs was with an organization in Philadelphia that sought to shut down crooked employment agencies that were secretly setting up brothels. They lured immigrant women into boardinghouses, sometimes drugging them and forcing them into prostitution. Perkins exposed 111 of these disguised brothels by applying for such jobs herself and confronting the pimps face-to-face.

Foremost motivation: please God

Perkins helped many people, but her first motivation was to please God. She described her work as a "deep vocation." "When a person gives a poor man shoes, does he do it for the poor man or for God? He should do it for God, she decided. *A person with a deep vocation is not dependent on constant positive reinforcement.* The job doesn't have to pay off every month, or every year. The person thus called is performing a task because it is intrinsically good, not for what it produces."[79]

Perkins endured decades of helping the needy because she wasn't depending on the immediate emotional rewards of her work, or the approval of people, which were so unpredictable.

Rejected by her colleagues

Perkins had a close relationship with President Roosevelt. When Roosevelt first invited her onto the cabinet, she refused, giving the excuse that there must be someone else more qualified. The President insisted that she was the right choice. Right from the start, Perkins let him know that she would be hounding him with the needs of poor Americans.

But Roosevelt did not always stand up for Perkins when she needed it. He was too slippery a politician to extend loyalty downward all of the time. She was not popular with many of the men in the cabinet. She was certainly not popular with the press.

As the years went by, she became exhausted by the job. Her reputation waned. Twice she sent Roosevelt a letter of resignation and twice he rejected it. In 1939 she became the target of impeachment proceedings. She was accused of being a communist by her own colleagues! The press coverage was brutal. Franklin Roosevelt was given a chance to rise to her defense but he didn't. He was wary of soiling his own reputation by association.

Perkins met with resistance on both ends—from the needy people she was helping, and from her co-workers in the government. She paid huge emotional costs in choosing a path of serving others.

Go to prayer
One way Perkins endured the crazy accusations of being a communist was by going to the All Saints Convent in Catonsville, Maryland for prayer and quiet. At the convent she would join in the communal prayer services five times per day. God was her refuge, her hiding place, and her strong tower of protection.

There were only two of President Roosevelt's closest aides who served with him for his entire presidency. Frances Perkins was one of them. She endured a long, trying career because she was not dependent on people's praise. She was living for an eternal reward.

How can you live a *whole life* of caring for others, even when they don't appreciate you? Jesus said, "Love your enemies." How can you possibly love people who hate you? You do it first as an offering to the Lord, knowing that he sees and appreciates it. You do it by the grace that God generously gives to anyone who humbly looks to him for help.

Dorothy Day
Dorothy Day was another example of a woman who was gripped by a calling to a vocation of serving people in need. She was a social activist, journalist and a leader in the Catholic Worker Movement in early 20th century New York. In her teens she "became converted to the poor, to a love for and desire to be always with the poor and suffering—the workers of the world." She served needy people until her early 80s. The key to her longevity in this work was to do it as an *offering of worship*.

Despite being an introvert, she worked for many hours a day caring for the poor. "She had a writer's personality, somewhat aloof and often craving solitude. But she forced herself to be with people, almost all day, every day. Many of those she served had mental disabilities or suffered from alcoholism. Bickering was constant. The guests could be rude, nasty, and foul-mouthed. Yet she forced herself to sit at the table and focus on the specific person in front of her. That person might be drunk and incoherent, but Day would sit, showing respect and listening."[80] The immediate rewards of working with hurting people are totally unpredictable. Dorothy Day shows us the way—she hung in there *no matter how she felt.*

At times, the guests would lavish praise on her. Receiving thanks for her service was like a rich feast for her soul. She had to work at not becoming proud when people praised her. "I have to stop myself sometimes," she wrote. "I have found myself rushing from one person to another—soup bowls and more soup bowls, plates of bread and more plates of bread, with the gratitude of the hungry becoming a loud din in my ears. The hunger of my ears can be as severe as someone else's stomach hunger; the joy of hearing those expressions of gratitude."[81]

For Dorothy Day, feeding the poor wasn't just an act of goodwill. It was an offering to God. She showed us that if all you do is an offering to the Lord, your kindness to others is pure. You don't require payback from people. When you are not yearning for "payback" for your kindness, you can give freely. If you have a "no-strings-attached" attitude with them, people can feel it. If they don't feel pressured to do anything in return, they're much more likely to enjoy your help. They don't feel like they're on the hook to repay you. If they are sensitive and socially in-tune, they will sense an open, gracious generosity. If they sense that you are at peace, they feel at ease. Your peace is infectious. But if your attitude is "I gave you this...now *you owe me,*" they will feel the pressure.

Brother Lawrence

Our third example of serving God in *all we do* is a very special monk from the 17th century—Brother Lawrence. We've seen in the lives of Frances Perkins and Dorothy Day that one of the great keys to serving

Living in Humility

joyfully in menial tasks is to do *all* our work *to and for the Lord*. Lawrence is another outstanding example of doing *everything in life* as an act of worshiping God.

Brother Lawrence was born around 1610 in France. He fought as a young soldier in the Thirty Years War, a conflict which involved most of the powerful nations of Europe. Over 8 million men died in this horrific war. Brother Lawrence was almost killed in this conflict and suffered heavy damage to his sciatic nerve. The injury crippled him and left him in chronic pain for the rest of his life. When his soldiering days ended, he entered into monastic life, beginning with a season in the wilderness living like one of the early desert fathers.

A few decades later, he entered a new monastery in Paris where he served as the cook for a community which grew to over one hundred members. He strongly disliked working in the kitchen. With chronic pain in his back and leg, his job was to cook everyday for a hundred hungry monks.

How did he live so peacefully in God's presence in this job? For years before this assignment, he had built a history of doing *everything* as an act of love for the Lord. He asked God for "grace to do his work well" and despite his disdain for kitchen work, he "found everything easy during his fifteen years of kitchen work." He hated working in the kitchen, but he was happy doing it because of the strong presence of the Holy Spirit in his life!

Lawrence shows us an amazing picture of humbly accepting the tasks put before us. When he accepted God's call to the monastic life, he trusted God to use his brother overseers to assign him the right tasks. He knew that whatever they asked him to do was God's will for him.

In first world countries, we often get to choose our occupation based on our preferences, skills and education. But in many other parts of the world throughout history, people have had very few options for work. Feeling *entitled* to enjoy our work is an attitude common to people in well-to-do countries. In third world countries, it's a different story.

Finding God in the kitchen

Brother Lawrence found the key to happiness while doing a job he disliked. He knew he was called to "Do it for the Lord, not for people." He shows us the right perspective: see your work as an act of worship. Continually give thanks as you work. Lawrence humbly accepted his job as a gift from God's hand and made the best of the situation.

Lawrence's habit of praying continually was so strong that he experienced no lessening of God's presence between praying alone in his room and working in a busy, crowded kitchen. That's amazing. "The time of busy-ness [in the kitchen] does not with me differ from the time of prayer. In the noise and clutter of my kitchen, while several persons are at the same time calling for different things, I possess God in as great tranquillity as if I were upon my knees at the Blessed Supper."[82] Wow!

"It was observed that in the greatest hurry of business in the kitchen, he still preserved his heavenly-mindedness. He was never hasty nor loitering but did each thing in its season with an even, uninterrupted composure and tranquility of spirit."[83] What a marvelous example Lawrence is. Every cup and spoon that you wash can be done as an act of love for God. You can clean up any mess left by your housemates with gratitude and peace, even if you're covering for someone else who has shirked their cleaning responsibility. Lawrence could have complained about his position. He could have asked for a higher position in the monastery. Instead, he found the peace of God in the job he naturally hated.

After fifteen years of working in the kitchen, his overseers transferred him to work in the monastery sandal repair shop. He went from cleaning dirty pots to fixing smelly sandals for one hundred brothers! And still he remained at peace.

Living in Humility

Continual worship

For Brother Lawrence, continual worship was the pathway to peace. In one of his letters to a friend, he wrote: "Do not forget Him but think on Him often. Adore Him continually. Live and die with Him. This is the glorious work of a Christian; in a word, this is our profession. If we do not know it, we must learn it."[84]

"God has many ways of drawing us to Himself. He sometimes seems to hide Himself from us. But faith alone ought to be our support. Faith is the foundation of our confidence. We must put all our faith in God. He will not fail us in time of need. I do not know how God will dispose of me but I am always happy."[85]

Brother Lawrence didn't know what new serving position he might be asked to do, but he *was* always happy. *Always happy,* even though he had chronic pain in his sciatic nerve from his war wounds. Humbly serving in a prayerful, trusting attitude was the key to his happiness.

You can do it with God's help

Frances Perkins, Dorothy Day and Brother Lawrence teach us to see our occupations as a deep vocation, a calling from God. Our service to people is all motivated by a root desire to love God.

The humility and dedication of these three shining examples enabled them to spend their whole lives serving a noble cause, even when rejected and mistreated.

Lord, we look to you for help. It is you who we serve and worship. Help us not to depend on the gratitude and compliments of those around us. Help us follow your example of pleasing your Father in all things. Holy Spirit, thank you for your presence in our lives. We invite you to be our guide, and to inspire all our words, actions and choices in life.

8

Living for God's Approval

"Your strength as an individual depends on how you respond to both criticism and praise. If you let either one have any special effect on you, it's going to hurt us. Whether it's criticism or praise, deserved or undeserved, makes no difference. If we let it affect us, it hurts us."[86]   John Wooden

People do the craziest things to get "views" and "likes" on social media. Recently there was a fad of kids eating pods of laundry soap just to get views on Youtube. Millions of people post videos to gain a following, to gain fans who will appreciate them and celebrate them in some way for their accomplishments, ideas, creativity, and their "look."

We crave attention and admiration. These days the hunger for fame has risen to new heights. In a 1976 survey that asked people to list their life goals, fame ranked 15th out of 16. But in a recent survey, 50% of young adults stated fame as a major life goal.[87] Early in her career, Madonna said, "I won't be happy until I'm more famous than God."[88] For many others, fame isn't the goal. But all of us want respect and appreciation from those closest to us, our friends, family and those in our circle of influence.

Living in Humility
___

We can become addicted to human praise, but God wants us to seek his approval. Jesus said, 'I always do what pleases him.'[89] Paul describes those who are fully dedicated to God: "Such a person's praise is not from other people, but from God."[90] When we live to please God, he "praises" us.

John's gospel tells us "some of the Jewish leaders believed in Jesus but they wouldn't admit it for fear that the Pharisees would expel them from the synagogue. For they loved human praise more than the praise of God."[91] We all have to decide whose praise we're going to pursue: the praise of people or God.

I grew up in Los Angeles, right down the road from Hollywood, the center of "show biz." The stars that work in Hollywood are the focal point of a gigantic amount of attention from around the world. Though I never tried to make it in show biz, I have the basic human condition common to us all. I like to be appreciated. After all these years of following the Lord, I still need to redirect my compass towards God's approval, not people's praise.

We can only rest in God
One of the most influential figures in church history is Augustine, born into an upper middle-class family in the year 354 in what is now Algeria. As a teenager, Augustine was a star pupil. A wealthy man named Romanianus recognized his potential and paid for Augustine's higher education. Augustine had an insatiable hunger to be recognized for his wit and debating ability. David Brooks wrote, "He is in love with the prospect of being loved. It's all about him."[92]

Many years later, around a decade after his baptism, he wrote his *Confessions*. All his striving for success and fame ended in frustration. He came to the conclusion that his only hope for fulfillment and peace was in knowing God. One of Augustine's best known quotes is: "You have made us for yourself, and our hearts are restless, until they can find rest in you."[93]

Like so many of us, Augustine tried his best to impress everyone, in hopes of becoming a star. But in that pursuit he found no rest, no *contentment*. No amount of human praise could satiate his hunger for significance. God kindly drew Augustine to himself and gave him peace. He realized that God had designed him to find his home, his rest and his contentment in knowing the Lord. If we are looking for praise in all the wrong places, we will not rest. God created us with a huge hunger to be loved. He is the only one who has enough love to fill this cavernous hole in our souls.

The faithful can be assured of God's approval

God is very consistent in noticing, appreciating and rewarding us for our good works! No act of kindness goes unnoticed by God. Even when you offer someone a cold cup of water, God notices.

Getting ready for worship leading can sometimes be a lot of work. I prayerfully plan the worship set, prepare and copy all the charts, contact all the band members, personally rehearse, learn a new song, and arrange how the songs are going to be played. Sometimes I set up a PA system, drum kit, and clean the rehearsal space. Often this is a volunteer, unpaid job.

My thoughts sometimes wander towards self-pity: "Wow, this is a lot of work! Why am I doing this!? The people I'm doing this for have no idea how much work it is!!" Then I remember, "O yeah, I'm doing it *for God*!" Serving the people is important, but firstly, this is my offering to the Lord. God sees it! He sees every little detail. I am doing *all of it* to the Lord. He sees all the sweat, all the frustration, all the hours that are completely hidden from everyone else.

What tasks do you work at behind the scenes? It might be hard labor, it might be childcare, and it might be doing tons of paperwork in a busy office. God sees your persistence and the steady faithfulness of your work. You may go unnoticed by any "important" people. But God sees your thoughtfulness, your prayerfulness, and the sacrifice of your comfort to help someone else. "Let us not become weary in doing good, for at the proper time we will reap a harvest if we do not give up."[94]

People disappoint us

If you live for human praise, you're setting yourself up for disappointment. Here's why.

Human praise is inconsistent. When we're around the same people for a long time, they grow accustomed to us and our gifts and strengths. Over time, people tend to show less appreciation for whatever value we're bringing.

Human praise is not strong or deep enough. In the year 2000 I had just finished a recording of my songs. The teenage son of a friend of mine had heard the CD. He offered me some weak praise for this project, "yeah, it's pretty good." It felt more like an insult than a complement. I was clearly overly sensitive to others' opinions of my new CD.

Sometimes we can read in a person's body language that they didn't like something we said, or some project or performance we delivered. It's disappointing. Sometimes it's what they *don't* say that bothers us. They make no mention of our work or whatever it is we're hoping they will notice. If you have an expectation of people always showing gratitude, you may end up resenting them, because getting praised by people is simply undependable.

Finally, there are *no eternal benefits* in human praise. These words of Jesus underscore how *important* it is to him that we are motivated by a desire to please *him*, not people. "Be careful not to practice your righteousness in front of others to be seen by them. If you do, you will have no reward from your Father in heaven."[95]

Jesus hammers home this truth: "you will have *no reward*" for doing good works for the wrong reason. "No reward" means *none*. Zero. That statement gives us every reason to examine our motives. What inward quality is produced by the outward habit of doing good works for the Lord instead of people? It builds into us loyalty, integrity, and humility. When you give to the poor, pray or fast, Jesus says, "do it in secret," not to be admired by people.

God promises to reward us for doing good

He will reward us for the good things we do. Jesus said, "I am coming soon! And when I come, I will reward everyone for what they have done."[96] This exact promise is repeated many times throughout bible history.

We receive both *present rewards* and *eternal rewards*. The immediate rewards we receive flow from a real, tangible experience of knowing God. We know his love, his peace, and his presence. He gives us assurance that we are his children. We are filled with a sure hope of heaven, not a "maybe this will happen" kind of hope. In this present life, we experience benefits such as freedom from anxiety about others' opinions of us, and God's empowering to accomplish tasks in trying times.

When Abram was on the road to the promised land, God said to him at one point, "Do not be afraid, Abram. I am your shield, your very great reward."[97] Knowing God is a huge reward. God's living word refreshes and gives joy to the heart.[98] Applying God's wisdom through hard work and good decisions also brings a present reward of provision.[99]

There is a lot we don't know about the nature of God's eternal rewards. But the things we do know are huge. We will feast with the Lord at the marriage supper of the Lamb.[100] He promises we will "reign with him."[101] We can be assured that "our light and momentary troubles are achieving for us an eternal glory that far outweighs them all."[102] We may not receive big material rewards in this life. But we see many tokens of God's love day by day.

Living in Humility

Living for long term rewards

Is it OK to be praised both by God and people? Yes, as long as our primary motivation isn't to garner human praise. Why do we so quickly gravitate towards finding our value from people instead of God? One reason is that rewards from people are often immediate. When people congratulate us, we feel it in our emotions and bodies. "Oh, what an amazing dinner that was!" "You look fabulous in that new dress!" "I was really impressed by your speech last night." Rewards from God are often delayed. We often have to wait for God to pay us back. The fruit of waiting is humility and faithfulness.

The praise you crave determines your ways

So far in this chapter, we've seen that loving human praise more than God's praise results in disappointment, anger, frustration and resentment. There is one other major problem—pleasing people can easily lead to compromise and sin. Out of a desperate desire to please people, we are tempted turn a blind eye to sin. The praise we crave dictates our behavior.

Today, the rejection of basic Christian beliefs and ethics is commonplace. It's politically correct to define your own sense of right and wrong—to do what's expedient instead of what's *right*. In a world like this, we're in big trouble if we are living for praise from the wrong people. This was the trap that King Saul was caught in, eleven centuries before Jesus was born.

King Saul

Saul was appointed king of Israel by God's chosen prophet, Samuel. But Saul severely lacked godly character. Out of a desire to please his followers, he tried to justify his disobedience to God. His conscience was seared by his lust for people's approval.

In the time of King Saul, Samuel was the national prophet of Israel. It was a different age of prophecy than we have now. *Everyone* knew that the anointed prophet spoke from God. He was highly respected. But Saul totally disregarded Samuel's instructions.

Saul was much more concerned with people's opinions of him than with God's opinion. He ignored the word of the Lord that came through Samuel. Samuel gave specific instructions that Saul and his army should kill the Amalekites and all their flocks and herds. Instead, Saul allowed the king to live, and he kept the livestock for his own people. For Saul, God's instructions seemed severe and pointless.

It's hard to understand why God would command that a whole people group be wiped out. I am not attempting to explain that. But the Amalekites had showed unrelenting savagery toward the Israelites for generations. God reminds the Israelites, "When you were weary and worn out, they [the Amalekites] met you on your journey and attacked all who were lagging behind." These stragglers would usually be women and children.[103] The Amalekites repeatedly destroyed the Israelites' land and food supply.

Saul simply did not humble himself to the Lord's instructions through Samuel. He thought he had a better idea than God. He had not learned to shut out the noise of the people around him and listen to God. Saul wasn't humble; he was proud and full of self-will. Saul's fear of people led to justifying his own sin.

Saul seeks his own honor
When he won the battle against the Amalekites, Saul was quick to celebrate his victory as his own accomplishment, to honor himself rather than God. After winning the war with the Amalekites, he went to Carmel to "set up a monument in his own honor."[104]

Saul was so self-deceived, that when the prophet Samuel showed up, he cheerfully greeted him, oblivious to his own sin. "May the LORD bless you," Saul said to Samuel. "*I have carried out the LORD's command!*" But he had *not* carried out the Lord's command! His pride had blinded him to doing what was right.

Saul was surrounded by a mob of soldiers who were famished with hunger after fighting a gruelling battle. They were likely saying to Saul, "Look at all these cattle! We could have the best barbeque ever! Let's do it!" Saul *feared* the opinion of his fighting men more than God's opinion, so he gave into them.

Blinded by his sin

John Wimber used to say: "Sin makes you stupid." If we are oriented towards gaining praise and approval from people, we shut out God's wisdom. We become blind to our own sin. Samuel confronted Saul by saying, "Although you were once *small in your own eyes*, did you not become the head of the tribes of Israel?" Being "small in your own eyes" is another way of saying *humble*.

Saul wasn't bowing to God's will, he wasn't making himself "small" before God. "Humility is simply seeing ourselves as we actually are, not higher nor lower. It means being gut-level honest about ourselves—being up front...It means living without hypocrisy."[105] Saul didn't do this. He lacked integrity. He did admit his error: "I have sinned. I violated the Lord's command and your instructions. I was afraid of the men and so I gave in to them."[106]

But his words of repentance were so shallow and insincere! "I have sinned. But please honor me (!) before the elders of my people."[107] The confession seems devoid of remorse. Saul wasn't concerned about displeasing the Lord. He wanted to be honored by his people. For Saul, his reputation was the most important thing. He had not developed a core conviction of God's ability to take care of him even though people opposed him. He was focused on the visible realm, not the invisible and eternal things.

The pressure to conform to worldliness today

In a time when it's popular to create your own philosophy, it's more important than ever to learn from the story of Saul. Again, we come back to the root issue: whose praise are you seeking? If you want to be admired by the "in crowd," you will be drawn into sinful choices.

I've watched my kids grow up in a much tougher world than I did. The temptations are now much more in-your-face than they were in the 1970s when I was a teen. In the information age, we can be sucked into all kinds of false pictures of "the good life."

God sees everything you do

How do we tear ourselves away from the addiction to people's opinions? There are three ways. One, get your emotional tank continually re-filled with love from God. Your life habits must include immersing yourself in the truth about God's love for you. God loves you unconditionally, wholeheartedly and continually.

If you're confident that God *highly regards you*, you don't ache for peoples' praise. Then you can *really* be free. You're no longer chained to people's opinions of you. You will be able to say as Augustine did, "You have made us for yourself, and our hearts are restless, until they can find rest in you."

Two, receive unconditional love from your church family. Become attached to a Christian community. You are one of the sons and daughters of our beloved Father. Find your sense of value from being intimately connected to the wonderful family of God.

Three, become convinced that God *sees* and will *reward* you for every good motive, thought and deed. Unlike humans, God is everywhere and he sees everything you do. Our Father "sees what is done in secret." He will reward you—you can count on it.

Living in Humility

"From heaven the Lord looks down...he watches all who live on earth—he who forms the hearts of all, who considers everything they do.[108] God promises us to reward us: "Anyone who wants to come to him must believe that God exists and that he rewards those who sincerely seek him."[109]

We play the long game. We know what counts in the end. It's not earthly plaudits and praises. It's the Father's approval. It's inheriting the kingdom of heaven, both now and in the next life.

As we wait for long-term rewards—over decades and a lifetime of faithfulness—we become more and more convinced that he loves us with an everlasting, affectionate love. I am motivated to honor God because I know he will reward and honor me in return.

9

Boast in the Lord

"You cannot exalt God and yourself at the same time."[110]
Rick Warren

"Humility is the displacement of self by the enthronement of God."[111] Andrew Murray

"A proud man is always looking down on things and people; and, of course, as long as you are looking down, you cannot see something that is above you."[112] C.S. Lewis

The humble heart is a grateful heart. Waking up in the morning and seeing green trees and a blue sky is an invitation to humbly say, "thanks for another day—thanks for creating beautiful things and letting me see them everyday." If we're occupied with worshiping and thanking God, we put down our pride. Worshiping God helps us gain perspective—everything good in life is a gift from God.

A memory of my early ego
I have a clear memory of leading worship one evening at a Langley Vineyard leaders meeting in the mid-1980s. The church was growing rapidly and had acquired a building. As the church grew, so did my own

Living in Humility

estimation of myself. As I was walking towards the platform to lead worship, I felt an impure sort of self-confidence and self-assurance. It's hard to describe: it's as if this self-centered, proud spirit was hanging on to me. All I could do was carry out my duty of leading some worship songs. Later, I had to ask God for forgiveness. Looking back on that moment, I feel my arrogant attitude, like a bad odor, must have been evident to some others in the room.

Because of a run of success in ministry, I had allowed pride to creep into my heart. Though I had been working on this heart issue for around ten years already, as my visibility grew, so did the temptation towards pride. I've thought of that little episode in my life many times. Seeing my own impurity was God's gift to me, to rescue me from myself. God, in his kindness, was leading me to repentance. He was saving me from an attitude of smug self-congratulation.

A quote from Augustine comes to mind. Augustine wrote in the 4th century, "Should you ask me what is the first thing in religion, I should reply, 'The first, second, and third thing therein.... no...all, is humility... If humility does not precede all that we do, our efforts are fruitless."[113] In this story of my early ministry, humility was not preceding all I was doing.

What do you do when God shows you your dark side? Do you quit your job and calling? No, of course not. You admit your mistakes and learn from them. This is one of the most important traits of humility. You *admit your need*. If we ask God, he will sensitize us to ugly things like pride. *Identifying* a problem is a huge step towards *solving* the problem. Awareness of our sin is one of God's gifts; it's his invitation to respond with confession. And he is always very quick to answer the prayer, "Lord, have mercy on me." His mercies are new everyday.

In knowing God, we get to know ourselves—the good and bad. We often need to ask God to help us examine our own hearts. We all need to frequently adjust our course towards true north. "Investigate my life, O

God, find out everything about me; Cross-examine and test me, get a clear picture of what I'm about; See for yourself whether I've done anything wrong—then guide me on the road to eternal life."[114] It seems to me I've prayed prayers like this thousands of times.

Don't Lose Perspective When You Find Success

The prophet Samuel said to Saul, "Although you were once small in your own eyes, did you not become the head of the tribes of Israel?"[115] Samuel implies that Saul is no longer small in his own eyes, but now has an inflated view of his own importance. It happens so easily. When we're successful, it goes to our head. We start believing what people say about us—"so talented...so smart...so gifted."

This is one big reason we need the spiritual disciplines. If we are looking into the mirror of God's word, we're reminded that every good gift comes down from our Father. So instead of giving in to pride, we give thanks. When your business is taking off like a rocket, profits are soaring, and the outlook is rosy for continued growth, watch out. Let your thanks to God flow. He's the one who gave you all your abilities, connections and education.

If you're a public presenter, beware of your enemy who looks for any opportunity to stumble you. He's a crouching lion, waiting to exploit any weakness he sees. When you're "killing it" in your presentations, look up to heaven. When people lavish on you praises for your eloquence, your wit, your voice, or your skillful leading, watch out. It goes to your head. It's time to *duck*. Bow to the one who has given you everything you have.

Remember the Indiana Jones movie where the guy seeking the treasure in the temple goes through a treacherous obstacle course and gets his head chopped off? It happened because he didn't read the instructions: "Duck." He forgot to keep his head low.

Living in Humility

After four decades of learning humility, my ego is still alive and well. The way to keep it down is to humble myself to God and others. The ego left unchecked is the cause of many businesses crumbling, marriages dissolving and churches falling apart.

Both Jesus and Paul showed us how to lay down our pride. They were two primary movers in a complete reversal of thought regarding humility and boasting in the ancient world.

Humility Revolution

In ancient Greek and Roman society, it was considered very acceptable to openly boast about your accomplishments. Whether you were the emperor or an average person, the very highest value in ancient Greek and Roman culture was *honor*. They didn't promote arrogance, but they believed that personal *merit* made you deserving of public *honor*. It was completely normal to go around town boasting about your achievements.

In fact, avoiding honor implied you weren't an honorable person. Lowering yourself before "the gods" or before the Roman emperor was considered right, but humbling yourself before someone of equal or lesser status was absolutely unheard of until the time of Jesus.

God-became-man did the unthinkable—he died in the most shameful way possible in First century society—by crucifixion. The idea of Jesus, the Messiah, lowering himself to a shameful death on a cross was ridiculous to the First century Roman mind. Paul says, "...the message of the cross is foolishness to those who are perishing, but to us who are being saved it is the power of God."[116]

Jesus and Paul show us the way—the humble way of dying to ourselves and living in God. Though our accomplishments may give us reason to boast, we boast only in the Lord.

Boast in the Lord

In Paul's second letter to Corinth, he facetiously says, "Since many are boasting in the way the world does, I too will boast." He begins by boasting of his pedigree as a Hebrew, but then lists all his many sufferings, beatings, hunger, sleepless nights in the cause of serving Christ and his church! He is boasting in his sufferings! Essentially, he is mocking the Greek and Roman tradition of boasting about their good deeds. "If I must boast, I will boast of the things that show my weakness."[117] Paul makes it clear—we prove ourselves by serving others, not by boasting.

Part of Paul's reason for writing on this topic was the "false apostles" who were infiltrating the church, masquerading as servants of Christ, but were only serving themselves. They self-confidently boasted in their spirituality.[118]

How to grow in humility

Jesus and Paul demonstrated a well-rounded practice of humility. It wasn't just a way of thinking, it was what they *did*. They both served the lowly. They both placed the needs of others before their own needs. They both chose to please God instead of themselves.

When I wash the dishes and clean the house, it helps purify my attitude. It keeps me from thinking I'm some kind of high and mighty patriarch. When I lead a musical worship time for a bunch of needy street people, most of whom aren't interested in worshiping God, it helps me develop a humble attitude. When I travel to a distant country, volunteering my time to encourage a new church plant, I remember that the Christian life is all about being like Jesus. It's all about laying down my life for those in need. You *learn* about Jesus and become more like him by *doing* Jesus stuff.

Worshipping God uproots pride

In worship, we meditate on how great God is. In comparison, we can't help but see how small we are. Seeing how puny we are in God's great universe, yet highly esteemed by God inspires us to worship him all the more! In worship, we take inventory of the great mercy God has shown us. We are reminded that the only reason we're welcomed to his table is by an undeserved gift of grace.

Bowing down keeps little worship leaders like me from thinking they are *really* something special. We realize we are special because he loves us. Worship points us towards an attitude of humble dependence on God. It keeps us from making big decisions without consulting the Lord. It keeps us from thinking we are God's answer to the world's problems.

Dallas Willard was a professor of philosophy at the University of Southern California and a prolific author. In this statement, Willard draws from the Romans 12 definition of worship: "Worship is the single most powerful force in completing and sustaining restoration of the whole person. . .Worship is at once the overall character of the renovated thought life and the only safe place for a human being to stand."[119] "Do not conform to the pattern of this world, but be transformed by the renewing of your mind."

Part of *renewing* our thinking is to *remember* where we were and who we were before we knew Christ. Paul is a great example in this respect. He remembers where he was when God called him—resisting Jesus.

"I thank Christ Jesus our Lord, who has given me strength...Even though I was once a blasphemer and a persecutor and a violent man, I was shown mercy because I acted in ignorance and unbelief. The grace of our Lord was poured out on me abundantly...Christ Jesus came into the world to save sinners—of whom I am the worst. But for that very reason I was shown mercy..."

Meditating on God's lavish mercy always pushes Paul towards worship! He finishes this section on God's mercy with a worshipful prayer: "Now to the King eternal, immortal, invisible, the only God, be honor and glory for ever and ever. Amen.[120]

Paul never forgets where he came from. Despite being a person who has seen miracles happen through his prayers, despite being lifted up to the third heaven, despite planting many churches and seeing hundreds or thousands of converts, Paul never forgets where he came from and the mercy God showed him.

When I remember all the ways God has lavished his grace on me, I'm so thankful. I was a self-serving teenager and God showed me his love. Along the way, he has shown incredible patience as I've slowly grown in his grace. He has accepted me despite my impure motives, kindly calling me to repentance. It's impossible to think of myself too highly when I remember God's constant grace for my sin.

Paul also visits this theme of overflowing mercy in Romans 11:
"For God has bound everyone over to disobedience so that he may have mercy on them all…Who has ever given to God, that God should repay them? For from him and through him and for him are all things. To him be the glory forever! Amen."[121]

Paul saw that God created us with full knowledge that we would disobey and disappoint him. He created us as dependent beings, needing his help to do what is right. *Every good thing we ever do* is only by God's grace. With this in mind, how can we possibly boast?

Paul knows in the depths of his heart that there is nothing he has ever been able to offer to God that God hasn't *already given him*! He knows that *all things* are *from* God and *through* God and *for* God. Paul keeps the mercy and grace of Jesus front and center. This keeps his ego down. To walk humbly, remember that "every good gift comes down from the Father of lights."

Avoid the hard thumps
One of the most gifted people in American history was Benjamin Franklin, a leading author, scientist, inventor and statesman in the 18th

Living in Humility

century. Franklin was endowed with many gifts—intelligence, creativity and diplomacy. As a teenager, Franklin learned an important lesson about arrogance and humility that always stuck with him.

In his book *Ego is the Enemy,* Ryan Holiday wrote, "In 1724, at the age of eighteen, a rather triumphant Benjamin Franklin returned to visit Boston, the city he'd run away from seven months before. Full of pride and self-satisfaction, he had a new suit, a watch, and a pocketful of coins that he spread out and showed to everyone he ran into—including his older brother, whom he particularly hoped to impress. All posturing by a boy who was not much more than an employee in a print shop in Philadelphia."[122]

During his stay in Boston, Franklin had a visit with Cotton Mather, a respected scientist, minister, and prolific author. The two were in Mather's home library, and when leaving the house, Mather warned Franklin not to hit his head on a low ceiling beam, calling out, "Stoop! Stoop!" Franklin didn't understand the warning and smacked his head on the beam. Mather took the opportunity to offer a word of advice. "You are young, and have the world before you; stoop as you go through it, and you will miss many hard thumps."

Years later, Franklin wrote of this experience to his son, "This advice, thus beat into my head, has frequently been of use to me; and I often think of it when I see...misfortunes brought upon people by their carrying their heads too high."[123]

Many times in life I've been too self-absorbed to avoid the hard thump. Through the years, I'm slowly learning to avoid the pain and disgrace of beating my own head against a big wooden beam.

The humble, grateful place is a safe place.

10

Wait Patiently for the Lord

I hate waiting. Waiting for a traffic jam to clear up, waiting on the phone to talk to an agent from the bank, waiting for my plane ride to end, waiting for someone to stop talking.

When you are a little child, you can't wait to be a big child. When you are a teenager, you can't wait to be an adult. When you have a bike, you can't wait to have a car. When you're a young adult, you can't wait to get married. When you are married, you can't wait to have kids. In a marriage, one spouse must often wait for the other to be ready to make a major life decision.

When you have an entry-level job you can't wait to have a promotion. When you get promoted you can't wait to have another promotion. If you have ministry gifts and aspirations, you can't wait for your big opportunity. When you have vision for reaching the next goal, you are always in the tension of waiting for the next step.

Life is full of waiting. Waiting patiently is one way God works humility into our lives. To wait patiently—whether it's 10 minutes or 10 years—is to admit we have no control over a situation. It's to say, "yes, God, you're here with me and I thank you for your blessings."

Living in Humility

Jesus waited

In waiting, we participate in the vulnerability of Jesus, who submitted himself to the frailty of the human condition. Jesus had to wait just like the rest of us. Just before Jesus turned the water to wine, he said some very strange things.

At the wedding in Cana, his mother asked him to solve a problem—the wine had run out. He responded by calling his mother, "woman," a very disrespectful term in his culture. He reacted to her like a petulant teenager, *"no* it's not my time!" And the very next moment, he *did* take care of the problem. That's very incongruent—he says, "no" and then he does it anyway. That's not how the Messiah acts unless something is troubling him.

Perhaps the explanation for this aberration in Jesus' behavior is that he was in the frustrating grip of *waiting for something very important.* Perhaps the wine at this wedding caused Jesus to think about the wine he would enjoy with his bride, the church, at the wedding supper of the Lamb. Meditating on this heavenly feast meant he was also thinking about the suffering he would have to endure before that glorious day. Jesus had to *wait* for the Father's timing to let his life, suffering, death and resurrection play out. Only then could he be united with his bride and taste the wine. (For a more in-depth look at this view of Jesus' first miracle-event, listen to the sermon, "Lord of the Wine," by Timothy Keller of Redeemer Presbyterian Church in New York City).

When we have to wait for something, we humbly accept that God is great and we are small. We patiently wait, trusting that he will bring good, though the waiting is painful. In a sense, the whole Christian life is about waiting to be clothed with our heavenly dwelling.

God forms us as we wait patiently. The process of waiting is the point, not just a pathway. He produces his likeness in us. He makes us a pleasing aroma as we humble ourselves in waiting for Him. Our friendship with him grows as we humbly submit to life's circumstances.

Learning to Get Low

Way back in the 70s when I started writing and recording music, God let me wait a decade before anything significant happened. This forced me to become grounded in knowing him. I went through the refining fire for a long time. Wait, wait, and wait some more. I was learning about humility.

When I first began, I was insecure, and very unsure of myself and my calling. I was trying to use my musical gifts while fighting off the ugly craving of self-exaltation. I often asked God to purify my heart and motives. Over the next 10 years, I received pastoral training and I wrote hundreds of worship songs. As I slowly grew in confidence and experience, I made a few attempts to share my songs with Christian record companies. Nothing came of it. More waiting. So I continued leading worship in my local church and occasionally led worship concerts in other churches.

Trust in the LORD and do good

In those days I was practicing the simple but powerful principle of waiting for the Lord: Psalm 37 says, "Trust in the Lord and do good; dwell in the land and enjoy safe pasture."[124]

Simply *do good.* Do good to your family, your church, and your community. It might be boring, or frustrating. It might seem like your dreams aren't coming true. That's OK, just *do good.* Don't try to be a hero, just do the right thing. A few verses later, the psalmist reiterates: "Be still before the Lord and wait patiently for him."[125]

I'm your typical firstborn "type-A" personality. I have a big roaring engine inside of me, driving me to achieve. After graduating from university, it was *very* humbling to have to wait several years for a career path to emerge. I was in the school of serving. I was a volunteer intern pastor in two different churches while working part-time, low paying jobs to make ends meet. I could have pursued any number of secular careers, but I felt called to Christian ministry and I couldn't settle for a different path. But what would my role in ministry look like? I couldn't see it. I had to *wait for it*.

As I waited, I was learning to love God and love people. I was learning not to be critical of other worship leaders who were less talented than I was. I was learning that the priority of life was to be loyal to God no matter what kinds of cards he was dealing me. I couldn't see a way forward so I had to do the obvious: keep my head low and use my gifts in the local church.

In 1985, ten years after beginning my spiritual journey, I moved to Canada to join the staff of a new church plant. Shortly after that, I was invited to lead worship at a conference led by John Wimber, the leader of the Vineyard movement and an internationally recognized speaker. Over the next 10 years, I led worship for dozens of large events with Wimber, all over the USA and internationally.

This was a big leap onto a much bigger platform. This was the beginning of a career as a writer, worship leader, recording artist and influencer of many other worship leaders. Since then, I've done a lot of waiting for other visions and plans to happen. Some have never happened because they weren't God's ideas. Some of them sputtered and died.

Through it all, I've learned to be content despite many unanswered questions. "A person's steps are directed by the Lord. How then can anyone understand their own way?"[126] Humble surrender is the way to wait patiently, and it's also the way to deal with a myriad of questions about life. He is God, we are not. Sometimes that means waiting.

He is your very great reward
Well into retirement age, Abram was visited by God. The Lord said to Abram, "Leave your native country, your relatives, and your father's family,

and go to the land that I will show you."[127] Abram's life is one of many examples of people called by God to do things they never would have chosen. They humbled themselves to obey God's will.

God decided it was time for an adventure of faith for the 75-year old Abram. Over the next 25 years, Abram journeyed with his wife, nephew and all his possessions to the far away land of Canaan. God made enormous promises to Abram—to make his descendants as numerous as the grains of sand in the earth. Abram had to wait a *very long time* for the promises to come true.

Abram left behind all that was familiar—the land of his father, and all attachments to his previous way of life. He became a sojourner, not knowing exactly where he was going. God appeared to him many times, reconfirming and expanding the promise of blessing. During the long wait, Abram's response (most of the time) was to keep on believing and keep on worshiping.

Abram encountered all kinds of difficulties and made some serious mistakes. He lied about his wife to foreign kings, saying Sarai was his sister instead of his wife. He lied out of fear that he and his people would be killed. God was gracious, rescuing Abram from the messes he got himself into. Despite lapses like this, God credits Abram for being faithful.

In one episode, Abram fought a battle to rescue his nephew, Lot, from local tribal chiefs. After this harrowing battle, the Lord spoke to Abram in a vision, "Do not be afraid, Abram. I am your shield, your very great reward."[128] God himself was Abram's reward. Ask yourself this question: "Do I look to God for my reward?"

On his journey to the promised land, Abram learned to put all of his trust and hope in God. While we wait for God's promises of blessing to materialize, we latch onto God as our reward. We deepen our loyalty to him and our friendship with him. In the waiting, we persevere and mature.

Living in Humility

We develop character. We walk by faith, doing the right thing even though we're still waiting for the promise. God is pleased by this.

Early in Abram's journey, God said to him, "Go, walk through the length and breadth of the land, for I am giving it to you."[129] It would be many years, perhaps two decades before the promise would be realized. Look at God's view of time in this passage: "...I am [*present tense*] giving it to you." Though it would be years before Abram received the promise, God said, "I *am* giving it to you." God has an elastic definition of time. He exists before time and outside of time. His ways are above our ways. We bow to his timing. Meanwhile, we wait patiently and live faithfully.

The world celebrates and honors people who exercise their personal power and prerogative; those who "take control of their own destiny." God applauds those who *wait patiently* for him to change their circumstances. Abraham's life is a picture of the marathon of faith that we walk. We steadily walk forward, often with many questions about why God is allowing us to face so many tests and trials.

The proud person says, "I demand answers!" when life is difficult. The humble person knows that "God is the potter and we are the clay." We allow him to continue shaping us according to his design and timing.

At the age of 99, God appeared to Abram, made a new covenant with him, and changed his name to Abraham. God repeated the plain and simple command, "I am God Almighty; walk before me faithfully and be blameless. Then I will make my covenant between me and you and will greatly increase your numbers."[130]

So many times, doing the plain and simple *right thing* is what is honoring to God. Like speaking the right words to our children or spouse, or workmates. Like continuing the same routine of being helpful and kind, one step at a time, one day at a time.

Waiting on the Lord while under attack

One of the toughest things I've had to wait for is deliverance from being attacked by friends who are acting more like enemies. When trusted brothers and sisters attack us, it's like a devastating blow to the solar plexus. I clearly remember several confrontations like this, sprinkled throughout the last 40 years. Church leaders who didn't agree with the decisions I was making. Heavy conflict with family members.

Sometimes, our friends can be downright vicious. Church members can hurl angry accusations, sowing discord and slander. Leaders in powerful positions abuse their power and sometimes the innocent are their target.

King David teaches us how to respond to attack. His life hung in the balance when political enemies and his own offspring turned against him. In Psalm 27, David is experiencing life-threatening danger. He runs to God for protection. Here is David's advice for those under attack: "Commit everything you do to the LORD. Trust him, and he will help you...Be still in the presence of the LORD, and *wait patiently* for him to act...Stop being angry! Turn from your rage! Do not lose your temper— it only leads to harm...Wait for the Lord; be strong and take heart and wait for the Lord."[131]

Wait, wait, and wait some more. Wait until God sorts out the craziness of being abused and accused. We must take the low place, not responding in the same angry spirit that is directed at us. God is our defender. *"Wait patiently* for him to act." If you are being wrongly accused, know that the truth will eventually become evident to all.

Jesus was the suffering lamb who went to the slaughter for our sake. He knows what you're going through. He is able to sustain you when your innocence is being questioned. Paul teaches the church in Rome how to love in the midst of conflict: "Bless those who persecute you; bless and do not curse...Do not repay anyone evil for evil...Do not be overcome by evil, but overcome evil with good."[132]

Living in Humility

We're not in control of the timeline of God's rescue from these attacks. All we can do is quietly go about our work, trusting that God will intervene. Don't let anger get the best of you. Keep your eyes on him with a trusting heart. Cling to the Lord who is "your very great reward."

At the age of sixty, I am always busy. There are plenty of ways to "do good, dwell in the land and enjoy safe pasture." As a free-lance worship leader / teacher, I'm frequently starting and finishing new assignments. While I'm busy with one thing I can see the end of the task a few months away. So, I pray and wait for the next thing.

In the past few months, as I see my current assignment coming to a close, he has been whispering to me, "there's something right around the corner...*wait for it*." While I wait, I try to treasure every day, enjoying each moment. I try to thank God for all his many blessings and make the most of every opportunity.

He is living inside you, enlightening your mind and speaking to your heart. His grace is empowering you for the next step. Abide in him, trust in him. Do good, enjoy safe pasture and be like Abraham—ready and willing to launch out on a new adventure of faith, no matter how young or old you are.

11

Humility Wins Hearts

"There is a universal respect and even admiration for those who are humble and simple by nature, and who have absolute confidence in all human beings irrespective of their social status."[133]
Nelson Mandela

People of diverse philosophies respect the humble. Those with a humble attitude will often find a pathway of favor open up before them in all kinds of situations. Though egotism is the modus operandi of many high profile rich and famous people, the virtue of humility is timeless and universally recognized.

In his bestselling book, "Good to Great," Jim Collins shared the findings of a study of 11 of the top Fortune 500 companies to determine what contributed to their great success. There were two main characteristics Collins found in CEO's who led their companies to great heights of success. The first was "ferocious resolve, and almost stoic determination to do whatever needs to be done to make the company great."[134] That's not surprising.

Living in Humility

The second trait Collins discovered in "good-to-great" CEOs is much more surprising: humility. Co-workers of these CEOs described them with words such as quiet, humble, modest, reserved, shy, gracious, mild-mannered, self-effacing, understated..." [135]

"The good-to-great leaders never wanted to become larger-than-life heroes." These leaders "channel their ego needs away from themselves and into the larger goal of building a great company...their ambition is first and foremost for the institution, not themselves."[136]

One such leader Collins studied was Darwin E. Smith. "In 1971 a seemingly ordinary man named Darwin E. Smith became chief executive of Kimberly-Clark, a stodgy old paper company whose stock had fallen 36% behind the general market over the previous 20 years. In the next 20 years Smith created a stunning transformation, leading Kimberly-Clark into the leading paper-based consumer products company in the world."[137]

It was an impressive performance... Yet few people know anything about Darwin E. Smith. "A man who carried no airs of self-importance, Smith found his favorite companionship among plumbers and electricians and spent his vacations rumbling around his Wisconsin farm in the cab of a backhoe, digging holes and moving rocks."[138]

Collins explains, "In contrast to the very *I-centric* styles of the comparison leaders, we were struck by how the good-to-great leaders didn't talk about themselves." The good-to-great leaders would deflect discussion about their own contributions. When pressed to talk about themselves, they'd say things like, "I hope I'm not sounding like a big shot."[139] Occasionally I run across a person who talks about nothing but himself for long periods of time. It's a test of my character to be around such people.

In his study, Collins developed a chart describing a hierarchy of leadership roles, the top being a "Level 5 Leader." This sort of leader is "never boastful" and "looks out the window, not in the mirror, to apportion credit for the success of the company—to other people, external factors, and good luck." They know they are part of team of contributors and are simply doing their part.

By contrast, there are famous, charismatic leaders like Lee Iacocca, who didn't handle great success with humility. Iacocca had a great start with Chrysler, saving this auto maker from near bankruptcy. He turned the company around and was a celebrated success. "Then, however, he diverted his attention to making himself one of the most celebrated CEOs in American business history."[140]

At one point, he considered running for president of the United States. He was once quoted as saying, "running Chrysler has been a bigger job than running the country...I could handle the national economy in six months."[141] Iacocca's early success led to a hugely inflated ego, and his company's success did not endure.

Katharine Graham
In 1963, Katharine Graham replaced her deceased husband as the publisher of The Washington Post. She was the first female publisher of a major American newspaper. Though inexperienced in business, Graham led this newspaper to tremendous growth and success.

Mrs. Graham entertained the rich and famous, including presidents and royalty from around the world. She was once asked, "What is the single most important trait of all great leaders?" Without hesitation, Graham said, "The absence of arrogance."[142] Graham saw arrogance as the one biggest factor in making a leader ineffective. Arrogance is defined as an "offensive display of superiority or self-importance; overbearing pride."

No one likes to be around people who consider themselves to be *superior*. Arrogance and pride drive people away while humility attracts them. If we embrace humility, we will eagerly listen to advice from our colleagues. We will naturally build relationships—in business, and all sectors of social life. It's easy to work with humble people because their priority is to respect, honor and serve others.

Socrates said, "The only true wisdom is knowing you know nothing." The humble know they will be stronger and more successful by listening to others' opinions. "Without good direction, people lose their way; the more wise counsel you follow, the better your chances."[143]

Jeff Boss wrote an article for Forbes Magazine called *13 Habits Of Humble People*. One of these habits is *They Listen*. Boss says: "There's nothing more annoying than being in a conversation with somebody who you can just tell is dying to get his or her words in. When you see their mental gears spinning, it's a sign they're not listening but rather waiting to speak. Why? Because they believe that what they have to say is more valuable than listening to you. In other words, they're placing their self-interest first."[144]

Boss observes the humble are good listeners: "Humble people, however, actively listen to others before summarizing the conversation. Moreover, humble people don't try to dominate a conversation or talk over people. They're eager to understand others because they're curious."[145]

Boss also notes the healthy, long-lasting relationships that exist between humble managers and their employees. He cites Jordan LaBouff's study of over 1,000 people, with around 200 in leadership positions. The study shows that "companies with humble people in leadership positions had a more engaged workforce and less employee turnover."[146]

Arrogant leaders
I imagine that Katharine Graham had seen many arrogant leaders who didn't listen well. They liked to talk only about themselves and their opinions. They couldn't hear constructive criticism from a subordinate or a colleague. In some cases, that attitude brought the downfall of a business.

In Jim Collins' *Good to* Great study, arrogance was a trait of most of the failed CEOs. "In over two-thirds of the comparison cases [failed companies], we noted the presence of a gargantuan personal ego that contributed to the demise or continued mediocrity of the company."[147] Arrogance blinds us to our own faults. It keeps us from entertaining the idea that our opinions might be wrong. That results in mediocrity in our own lives and in the organizations in which we work.

This truth is echoed by Maria Bartiromo a successful financial journalist who has worked with CNN, CNBC and Fox News. Bartiromo wrote a book called *The 10 Laws of Enduring Success*. She wrote: "Without humility, you can never see the truth about yourself and others."[148]

Bartiromo joins the chorus of those who are impressed by the humble: "Some of the greatest people I know are also the most humble. Humility doesn't mean being wishy-washy, or letting others run over you in their climb to the top. It's merely the understanding that you're human...."[149] She argues that humility is attractive: "People with humility are extremely appealing.... We enjoy it when people can laugh at themselves. We dislike finger-pointers and sentence parsers—those who are always looking out for their image."[150]

Pat Williams is an author and motivational speaker and has held many top level sports executive positions in the NBA. In his many years of leading successful professional sports teams, Williams has learned a lot about the value of humility: "Humble leaders are strong enough to listen to other points of view, strong enough to admit mistakes and learn from them, strong enough to celebrate the achievements and successes of others, and strong enough to surround themselves with talented people without feeling threatened or diminished."[151]

People are drawn to humility

A brief look into history shows that people such as Abraham Lincoln and Benjamin Franklin embraced humility, and it was a key to their success. In secular society, the idea of *humility* may not be talked about much, but people notice and respect this quality. It's like a spiritual law that works for all kinds of people. If you are kind, attentive, and willing to learn, you will gain favor with people. Humility makes you *likable.*

Here is what C.S. Lewis has to say about the profile of a humble person: "Probably all you will think about him is that he seemed a cheerful, intelligent chap who took a real interest in what you said to him. If you do dislike him it will be because you feel a little envious of anyone who seems to enjoy life so easily. He will not be thinking about humility: he will not be thinking about himself at all."[152]

Why would Lewis describe a humble person as *cheerful?* What is the connection between humility and cheerfulness? Humility is one of a family of character traits. The humble person chooses to let God into every area of life. The humble person entrusts everything to God and is therefore not ruled by anxiety. The humble person makes an effort to think about things that are true, noble, right, pure, lovely, admirable and excellent. This kind of thinking invites joyfulness into our lives. By contrast, if all you ever think about is yourself, you'll find a thousand reasons to be unhappy. In Christ, we learn to be joyful even in difficulty.

Humble people are not dour, sour types. Lewis describes the humble person as *interested in others* because that is exactly what real followers of Jesus are like. Knowing Jesus turns our gaze outward to those around us. You become a good listener when you "consider others more important than yourself." When you're listening intently, people feel that you genuinely care about them. Lewis describes the humble person as *one who enjoys life* because abiding in Jesus frees us from anxiety and gives us a positive outlook.

In his book, *Humility: The Secret Ingredient of Success*, Pat Williams says: "There are few experiences more enjoyable than meeting a truly humble person. When you are in the presence of humility, you know that you will be received, listened to, and accepted for who you are. A truly humble person won't try to impress you, manipulate you, judge you, criticize you, or put you in your place. Humble people are safe to be around. You can relax. You can be yourself."[153]

No guarantees
While living humbly doesn't guarantee any specific reward or promise of success, it puts you in a position to receive whatever blessings God may have in store for you. There are countless examples of this from history—stellar examples of humble people that can be described as successful, both in God's eyes and by societal standards.

We can't isolate a specific causal effect between doing a good deed and receiving a certain blessing, whether it's a material gift or a spiritual one. But it's clear that humble people are more likable. With humility comes an assortment of other character qualities: love, kindness, patience. The humble person honors and forgives others and isn't boastful or envious of others. These qualities describe a person who is a delight to have in your place of work, or your church or home. In many cases, doors of opportunity open up to humble people because they "shine like stars in the sky."[154] Humility is not a means to an end, it is an integral part of becoming more like Jesus. And it often brings earthly rewards.

It's also clear that some people struggle greatly in life despite their humility. Bad things happen to humble people. The names of some of my friends come to mind. They are faithful, humble Christians who have traveled a very rugged road in life. The cause of their hardship may be an unfaithful spouse, a fatal sickness or a tragic accident. They struggle to find employment or have little fruit in their ministry efforts. Though we can't understand why one person runs into more problems than another, we can be assured that in the long run of eternity, God will reward us for what we've done.

Every Christian is blessed by God but will also experience difficulty. Some experience greater tragedy and hardship than others. The list of heroes of the faith in the 12th chapter of the book of Hebrews is testimony to the truth that humility doesn't always lead to being accepted. For the martyrs, humility led to being killed for their faith. Proverbs tells us: "True humility and fear of the Lord lead to riches, honor, and long life."[155] There are many examples of this in modernity and in history. But we can also point to many examples of humble people who weren't rich or honored by their peers or blessed with a long life. There are other kinds riches that are worth much more than money. Rich relationships come to those who walk in humble love—those who are patient and undemanding instead of jealous, boastful and proud.

The divine spark of humility in all of us
Throughout history, we see notable people who are humble, and aren't necessarily Christians. God has made all people in his image. Each of us is born with a potential for humility. By the spark of divine life in us, humans have the capacity to learn virtuous things before recognizing Jesus as God. God generously pours his wisdom into the heart that seeks to do right.

Many non-Christians are in touch with their God-implanted yearning for eternity, so they pursue virtuous lives. If they can do it, how much more can we who are filled with God's Spirit do it! God is not stingy with his grace. There is plenty of it to go around. All it takes is a soft heart and a listening ear to grow in humility. He is with you, in you and all around you. He is constantly ready to reveal himself to you, that you might reflect more and more of his glory and humility.

Humility opens doors
Humble behavior creates a pathway, opens doors and leads to success in life because no one wants to hire an arrogant snob. Those genuinely interested in the well being and prosperity of others attract friends and clients. People are more apt to listen to your sales pitch if you are a caring,

gracious person and you're motivated by a genuine desire to *help* your clients.

In your day-to-day setting, the people around you have the ability to recognize humility. No matter how old or young, how religious or non-religious, people can feel it when someone is genuinely interested in them. People will sense an openness and generosity of heart.

When you give others credit when it's due, they take notice. If you never brag about your accomplishments, they take notice. If you are quick to listen to others for advice instead of dismissing them, they take notice. If you are surrounded by talented people and you celebrate their contributions to your group, people will like being around you. If you consider others more important than yourself, they will feel respected and valued by you.

The world is changed one conversation at a time by common, everyday people who are loving and humble. You can do it with God's help.

12

Grace for Going to the Margins

Bishop of the Slums

I love the story of a priest named Bergoglio. Before entering seminary to study for the priesthood, he worked as a night-club bouncer, a janitor, a chemical technician, and a literature teacher. This Argentinian priest was unusual. At night, he spent much time walking the streets, looking for the wounded and hungry. He helped them find food, shelter and healing.

In some of the toughest neighborhoods of Buenos Aires, he waged a war against drug addiction, establishing many recovery and educational programs to rid people of bondage to "Paco," a cheap and dangerous form of cocaine. He oversaw the establishing of Hogar de Cristo, a rehab center, and two farms dedicated to getting addicts back on their feet. The ex-addicts were given opportunities to gain new work skills by apprenticing to become electricians, stonemasons or metalworkers.

After serving for 53 years, as a priest, teacher, administrator and bishop, Bergoglio was elected as pope of the global Roman Catholic church in the year 2013. He is loved by people from all walks of life, all religions and all nations. Attendance at Catholic churches has surged in many nations as a result of his influence. He is known for creating a more inclusive and open Church focused on meeting the needs of all people.

Living in Humility

When a bishop is chosen to be the Catholic Pope, he chooses a name for himself. Bergoglio chose the name Francis, after St. Francis of Assissi. St. Francis was known for ministering to the poor, sick and weak. Bergoglio's years of working with the needy shaped him into the man we see today, who invites groups of homeless people to share meals at the Vatican...the man who washes the feet of prisoners (both men and women) and embraces sick and disfigured people that most of us would be afraid to touch.

Pope Francis is like Jesus in many ways. He chooses to be *with the poor*, not just study and talk about them. He says, "When it comes to social issues, it is one thing to have a meeting to study the problem of drugs in a slum neighborhood and quite another to go there, live there, and understand the problem from the inside and study it.... [O]ne cannot speak of poverty if one does not experience poverty, with a direct connection to the places in which there is poverty..."[156]

A phrase that Pope Francis often speaks to leaders is, "smell like your flock." This means, "spend time with the people under your care," whether it be your business, or a church. Bergoglio hung around with drug addicts for many years and is comfortable dining with these people even in his position as pope.

Soon after becoming pope, Francis gave orders to one of his archbishops to continue the work he could no longer do: "You will not stay behind a desk signing parchments," the Holy Father told the archbishop. "Now I want you always among the people. In Buenos Aires, I often went out in the evening to go find the poor. Now I no longer can. It is difficult for me to leave the Vatican. You will do it for me."[157]

Staying Low
Francis is a refreshing example of a powerful person who has chosen a humble path. He shuns the traditions of royal treatment given to the long

line of Catholic popes that precede him. He takes the public bus, lives in a modest apartment, and still prepares some of his own meals. He doesn't like to be lifted up on high platforms above everyone else. He likes to sit at round tables to have discussions with the common folk, eagerly listening to their views on all sorts of issues.

But Francis is far from simple—he has a keen intellect and is unafraid to confront the status quo. He has the same Spirit of Jesus, who upset the money changers' tables in the temple area because they were hindering the poor from worshiping God. Pope Francis confronts religious systems and practices that have strayed from the heart of God.

In his book, *A Big Heart for God...* he says, "I dream of a church that is a mother and shepherdess. The church's ministers must be merciful, take responsibility for the people and accompany them like the good Samaritan, who washes, cleans, and raises up his neighbor...."[158] Francis' actions and teachings echo the story of the Good Samaritan: it's not just about what you *know*, it's what you *do* that counts. Pope Francis follows the example of Jesus: make it a priority to leave behind your place of privilege to help the needy.

Jesus' Humble Station

It is said, "The medium is the message." Through Jesus, the Father's message is this: he cares for the "little guy" *so much* that he sent his Son to be one of them. He has a bias towards helping the poor. This theme runs prominently throughout both the Old and New Testaments. Between his humble birth and his shameful death, Jesus was a member of a low-income family. His highest priority was to help wounded, weak, sick and poor people. He said, "Healthy people don't need a doctor—sick people do."[159]

The incarnate Christ came not only to *help* the needy, he came *as a needy person*. He wasn't a down-and-out dropout, but he wasn't in the upper echelons of society either. None of us regular humans can truly grasp the significance of this gigantic downward step taken by the pre-

Living in Humility

existent cosmic Christ. The Messiah came as a common man, for the common folks.

Jesus grew up in Nazareth, a humble little no-name town. When someone said Jesus was from Nazareth, they shouted back, "Nazareth! Can anything good come from there?"[160] Nazareth was a backwoods place where poor people lived.

Jesus' parents could afford only the cheapest possible offering at his baby dedication service. They offered either "a pair of doves or two young pigeons" because that's all they could afford. The law allowed the poor to make this type of inexpensive offering.[161] Jesus came from the poor side of the tracks. It's possible that Joseph and Mary struggled to make ends meet because the community shunned them for having an "illegitimate" child.

Everything about Jesus was humble—his birth, his family of origin, his economic status, and his reputation. He didn't show up on the scene in a golden chariot. He was a simple peasant. He usually called himself "Son of Man," which means a *human being,* with an emphasis on weakness and frailty.

During his public ministry, we never see Jesus lacking food. He had a group of supporters who took care of him. But he didn't live a luxurious life in a mansion or private mountain retreat. He didn't have his own home. He slept on borrowed cots on the ground. He looked and dressed like a regular guy. He wasn't handsome. He didn't look like the Messiah that people were hoping to see.

His name in Hebrew was Joshua, a very ordinary name, like "John" or "Jim" in today's world. Because he was born to a woman out of wedlock, some would have called him "bastard child." His ancestral line was filled with people who did bad things. Rahab was a prostitute, Jacob was a cheater and David was an adulterer and murderer. Before he began healing the sick, his status in the neighborhood was very unimpressive. In most respects, Jesus was an average guy in his community. Because of all this, the average person could identify with him. Jesus was touchable, available, and vulnerable.

Jesus' Top Mission
After Jesus was tested in the desert, he "returned to Galilee in the power of the Spirit."[162] Immediately, news spread about Jesus throughout the countryside. In our day, when we hear the phrase "in the power of the Spirit," it is usually connected to church meetings where God speaks through a preacher and maybe heals some people. Jesus prioritized his use of power by hitting the streets and helping the poor to get back on their feet.

On his first Sabbath day of public ministry, he spoke in the synagogue. When the leader of a movement makes his first public statement of purpose, he wants to give the clearest possible picture of who he is and what he's about. On this day at the synagogue, Jesus made clear what his top priority was. He read his mission statement from Isaiah 61: "The Spirit of the Lord is on me, because he has anointed me to proclaim *good news to the poor*. He has sent me to proclaim freedom for the prisoners and recovery of sight for the blind, to set the oppressed free..."[163]

Paul reminds us that Jesus, "though he was rich, yet for your sake he became poor, so that you through his poverty might become rich."[164]

When John the Baptist was in prison, wondering whether he had gotten it right by identifying Jesus as the "Lamb of God," he sent a message to Jesus, asking if he was "the one." Jesus replied, "The blind receive sight, the lame walk, those who have leprosy are cleansed, the deaf hear, the dead are raised, and the good news is proclaimed to the poor."[165] "Here is the proof that I am the one," Jesus was saying to John. This is what the kingdom of God looks like: the sick and poor are helped and rescued.

He showed us the upside-down kingdom—where the big boss is doing the grunt jobs. The last person he thinks of is himself. He's always shocking his closest friends by doing the opposite thing they expect a Messiah to do. Giving away tons of free food. Hanging out with a woman from a despised religious sect called the Samaritans!

Do this and you will live
In the story of the Good Samaritan, the expert in the law came to Jesus with wrong motives. He knew that loving God and neighbor were the most important things. But his definition of "neighbor" was very narrow. He felt fine about helping the people who lived in his neighborhood, but the idea of helping a lowly Samaritan was repulsive to him. In Jesus' story, the Samaritan is the hero because he does something to help someone in dire need. Jesus says to the Bible expert: "Do this and you will live."[166]

These words of Jesus bring to mind a quote from Mother Teresa, "A life not lived for others is *not* a life." Wow, what a great paraphrase of the words of Jesus. If you live only for yourself, focused on your own needs, your life will wilt and shrivel. The way to *find* your life is by giving your life away.

How do we apply this to our lives? First, don't be overwhelmed by the millions of needs in the world. You don't have to be the next Mother Teresa. But listen to Mother Teresa's wise advice: "Do not think that love in order to be genuine has to be extraordinary. What we need is to love without getting tired. Be faithful in small things because it is in them that your strength lies... Not all of us can do great things. But we can do small things with great love."[167]

It's not about being a hero, it's about stepping forward into faithfulness, one day at a time. Pope Frances said, "If we can develop a truly humble attitude, we can change the world,"[168] The pope influences millions but he's in a very unique position.

Mother Teresa's words are so practical: "If you can't feed a hundred people, feed just one. Never worry about numbers. Help one person at a time and always start with the person nearest you."

Everyone can share
Mookie Betts is one of those people who fed the hungry people near him. Mookie was the American League Baseball batting champion in 2018. On October 24, in the second game of the World Series, millions of people watched Mookie and his team win another game. A few hours after the game, around 1 a.m., Mookie and his cousin went on a secret errand of mercy.

Wearing hoodies that covered most of their faces, they took dozens of trays of food to the freezing homeless community congregating around the public library in Boston. When Mookie realized someone had recognized him, he quietly walked away before anyone could take his picture. Mookie was simply doing what he could do, with the time and resources God had given him. He didn't do it for a photo-op, he did it because it was the right thing to do.

Jesus' heart burned with compassion for the "sheep without a shepherd." The outcasts and destitute knew he was genuinely concerned for them. He honored the poor widow, saying her small gift was "more than all the others." He taught us to invite the poor to dinner and make sacrifices to share our resources with them. Ask God for more of his heart of compassion for the suffering people who live on the margins of society. Be touchable, available, and vulnerable. Be kind to those who struggle, to those who have little or no resources by virtue of their family of origin.

To learn humility is to watch Jesus and do what he does. Catch his heart—be happy to talk to and help anyone regardless of their background. Listen for the Holy Spirit's nudges. He will show you how to use your unique relationships, resources and creativity to help someone near you.

13

I Can't Believe You Said That!

"Overlook an offense and bond a friendship; fasten on to a slight and – good-bye, friend!"[169] *Proverbs 17:9*

Well-meaning people sometimes say shocking, insulting things. Often, they don't realize they're hurting us. We all have blind spots. Sometimes we don't realize our words are like daggers to the heart. It's not just insensitive, self-centered people who offend us. It's also the caring people we love and respect. In those moments of insult, we are tempted to borrow a line from a Harry Potter movie: "Once again, you show all the sensitivity of a blunt axe."[170]

Has anyone ever insulted your appearance? Insulted your abilities? Insulted one of your family members, maybe one of your children? And sometimes, you could tell that they had no idea how inappropriate their comment was? You feel like saying, "I can't believe you said that!" It doesn't feel good. It makes you angry. When those kinds of comments are made, you have a choice. You stand in the valley of decision. You feel like slapping them in the face but you know you shouldn't. You could retaliate with an "eye for an eye" or...pause and let your temper cool down. Thank God that he is really *with us* in those moments to help us consider what to say, if anything at all.

Lincoln's humble response to insult

Here is an astounding example of humility in the face of insult from the life of one of the earliest presidents of the United States, Abraham Lincoln. Lincoln wasn't a self-serving politician. He was truly a servant of the nation's population. He was highly committed to liberating all the slaves in the Southern United States. This led to the Civil War between the North and South. He had the odious task of managing the country throughout this horrible war that claimed the lives of over 600,000 soldiers.

Lincoln's commitment to ending the war as swiftly as possible required him to work with some very arrogant military generals. He respected these generals for their military prowess, but sometimes the feeling wasn't mutual.

Lincoln appointed Edwin Stanton to be his secretary of war. He did this despite Stanton's intense animosity towards him. "Stanton hated Lincoln, calling him a 'low, cunning clown,' a 'gorilla,' and a man of 'painful imbecility.'"[171] Because of Stanton's horrible record of insulting Lincoln, he could hardly believe it when the man he so harshly insulted offered him this prestigious position in government.

One day, Lincoln sent a note to Stanton, suggesting a certain course of action in the ongoing civil war. Stanton's reaction was to say, "Lincoln is a fool." Lincoln predicted this arrogant response, but his response was amazingly humble. He said to the messenger who brought Stanton's reply, "Well, if Stanton said I was a damn fool, then I must be one, for he is nearly always right, and generally says what he means. I will slip over and see him."[172]

This was the reaction of the President of the United States to being called a "fool" by one of his top aides! He would have been justified in firing Stanton immediately. But he didn't pull the "You're Fired" trigger on Stanton. He knew that wouldn't be the best choice for his country. He knew Stanton was an effective leader despite his rude behavior. Lincoln didn't let his temper get the best of him. He didn't send an angry memo summoning Stanton to his office. Instead, he took the humble road, walking to Stanton's office to talk it over.

Another general, George B. McClellan, treated President Lincoln equally as badly. McClellan's treatment of Lincoln was so bad, it was reported in the newspapers. But Lincoln tolerated the abuse, saying, "I will hold McClellan's horse, if he will only bring us success."[173] Lincoln wasn't thinking of himself, his feelings, or his position over these generals. He was thinking of minimizing the loss of human life—saving the lives of young soldiers. He emptied himself of selfish pride and ego for the good of the country.

Lincoln's humble attitude is strikingly different from some who are in powerful positions today. Often we hear of an insubordinate employee being "fired" by their overseer. Lincoln was very slow to made these kinds of decisions. He was willing to work with people who were a constant irritation if it they had valuable skills that helped the nation.

Humility is having power and not using it until the right time and opportunity. "Better to be patient than powerful; better to have self-control than to conquer a city."[174] Abraham Lincoln endured mistreatment for the sake of others and surrendered his right to retaliate. He held one of the most powerful positions in the entire world, but he laid down his power for the sake of the suffering soldiers and the nation. Lincoln said, "Nearly all men can stand adversity, but if you want to test a man's character, give him power." Lincoln is a stalwart example of a man who used power with humble self-restraint.

Lincoln's example shows us another sister-trait of humility is *mercy*. When you know that you've *received* a lot of mercy, you freely give it. Lincoln was amazingly merciful to people of every rank, social status, color and creed. He personally helped the lowest ranking soldiers in the war and showed undeserved kindness to pompous military generals.

Living in Humility

John Ruskin, a prominent British social thinker and philanthropist in the Victorian era, said: "I believe that the first test of a great man is his humility. I don't mean by humility, doubt of his power. But really great men have a curious feeling that the greatness is not of them, but through them. And they see something divine in every other man and are endlessly, foolishly, incredibly merciful."[175]

Insults are opportunities to grow
When someone insults me, if I'm tracking with the Holy Spirit, I usually just smile. I usually can't think of anything except fighting words. So I try to practice something my mother taught me: "If you can't think of something nice to say, don't say anything at all."

Once in awhile, I mess up and lash out in anger. When I blurt out a defensive comment, later I always wish I had kept my mouth shut. Sooner or later I have to apologize. It helps me to think of Jesus, the most unjustly insulted and mistreated person in the history of the world. The perfect Son of God, who loved the lowest, fed the hungry, healed the sick and humbly served his friends. He was mocked, beaten, spit upon and crucified because he told the truth.

Any mistreatment I've ever received pales in comparison to the violence leveled against Jesus. He didn't deserve it! Bad things happen to all of us that we don't deserve. Bad things happen to good people. How are we going to react? With our jaws jutting and our fists outstretched or with meekness?

We belong to the upside-down kingdom of God. The King of this kingdom said, "Blessed are the meek, for they will inherit the earth."[176] One definition of meek is to be like a mighty stallion who has been trained to follow his master. We have the power to overwhelm, but in submission to our Master, we humble ourselves and wait for instructions. Jesus says if we walk this way, we will do really well in life—we will inherit the earth.

I Can't Believe You Said That!

Maybe God allows insulting words to be shot out of people's mouths like an arrows into our souls because he wants to give us a chance to practice forgiveness. Mother Teresa said, "There are a few ways we can practice humility...To pass over the mistakes of others. To accept insults and injuries. To accept being slighted, forgotten and disliked. To be kind and gentle even under provocation."

Overcoming our over-sensitivity

Getting insulted also gives us a chance to examine if we are overly sensitive. Maybe those words *feel* like an insult because we have a raw spot in our soul that needs healing. When mistreated, we press into our Father's love for us where we find comfort and healing. In that place, nothing can touch us.

Mother Teresa said, "If you are humble nothing will touch you, neither praise nor disgrace, because you know what you are." Being insulted drives us back to God's unchanging, solid-rock love.

If we allow cutting words to get down deep into our psyche, we may find ourselves privately constructing arguments and comebacks to our attacker. We may be so upset that we wake up in the middle of the night, planning our counter-attack.

That's when we know it's time to let go, forgive, and ask for God's blessing on that person. Do you want to go to jail? That's what Jesus says will happen if you don't forgive. You'll get thrown into a dungeon of torment if you refuse to forgive.[177] Those are the words of Jesus! No, that person that hurt you doesn't deserve to be forgiven, but neither do you. It's you who will be hurt if you don't forgive. Nelson Mandela said, "Resentment is like drinking poison and then hoping it will kill your enemies."

Jesus forgave us a debt we could never repay, and he asks us to do the same for others. He enables us to forgive. Sometimes we may pray, "I forgive Sarah" and we don't *feel* an ounce of love. That's OK. Praying that prayer, even if you can barely get the words out, is a good beginning. To forgive is to humble yourself. It's to say, "I'm not going to retaliate even though I feel like you deserve punishment. I'm not going to use my power to take you down."

Don't return evil for evil
In the Ancient Near East, it was legal for you to pursue vengeance or retaliation, equal to the offense. "An eye for an eye, and a tooth for a tooth."[178]

You could take something of equal value from someone to replace what they took from you. But, Jesus says even if the law allows you to do this, don't do it. If you do, it will destroy any chance of relationship with that person. Don't insist on being paid back. Instead, be willing to suffer being wronged. Lay down your power.

Vulnerability
Jesus made himself absolutely vulnerable. Will we trust him enough to follow his example of vulnerability? Sociologist Brené Brown says, "Vulnerability is the birthplace of love, belonging, joy, courage, empathy, and creativity. It is the source of hope, empathy, accountability, and authenticity. If we want greater clarity in our purpose or deeper and more meaningful spiritual lives, vulnerability is the path."[179]

Vulnerability is the way to genuine relationship. We can't love or be loved unless we're vulnerable. We can't belong to a group of close friends unless we're vulnerable. We can't be all we were made to be unless we're built into relationships through vulnerability. People can trust us if they see that we've laid down our power. God meets us in our vulnerability. He dwells with the contrite and humble. He draws near to the humble and opposes the proud.

Do what Lincoln did

It comes down to this: will we lay down our pride for the good of the whole group? For Lincoln, there was no question whatsoever. He was willing to take *any insult* if it would only bring healing to his war-torn country.

Are you willing to let go of your opinions, your preferences, your side of the argument in order to make peace? If you want a meaningful relationship with your spouse, children or coworkers, you need to make yourself vulnerable. You need to be open, teachable and ready to listen and learn from everyone around you.

This is what I've done in my 37 years of marriage, and I still have to work at it. Because Linda and I have refused to be entrenched in self-absorbed attitudes, we have a strong marriage. A broken relationship is a non-option for us, so we humble ourselves to one another.

In positions of authority, it's easy to criticize. Our observation about a person's faults may be *true* but it may not be helpful to tell them about it. Power can be used to build up or tear down. Words can build up or destroy. Don't let careless words set fire to your friendships.

Lincoln saved his country by his self-sacrificial humility. Maybe you'll get a chance to save your marriage, your family, your church or your business by taking the humble road.

Yield to love! God is love, and he's living inside you! If you surrender to his love, you'll eventually be saturated with an awareness of his love. Then, it's not so hard to let go of your pride.

14

I Don't Like that Shade of White

"...where He is enthroned in the heart, His humility and gentleness will be one of the streams of living water that flow from within us."[180] Andrew Murray

"All of you, clothe yourselves with humility toward one another, because, "God opposes the proud but shows favor to the humble."[181] 1 Peter 5:5

A few summers ago, we put a fresh paint of coat on the walls of our house. We tested small samples of a few different shades of white and decided on a color. After a few trips to the paint store and some experimenting and discussion, I paint-rolled and cut in the first coat of paint in the hallway.

My wife said, "I don't like that shade of white." As I felt my anger and frustration beginning to boil, I said to myself, "Hmmm, should I die on this hill or just let her have her way?" After some disgruntled discussion, I made the smart choice and let her pick yet another new shade of white.

This example of arguing over paint color may seem silly. But it's in these ordinary situations that humility will make a big difference. "The only humility that is really ours...is that which we carry with us, and carry out in our ordinary conduct; the insignificances of daily life are the tests of eternity, because they prove what really is the spirit that possesses us."[182]

In marriage and in *all* relationships, letting other people *have their way* is often the right choice. After all, how big a deal is the shade of white on your walls? (We call that a "first-world problem" in our house. In many other countries, people can't afford a house, let alone new paint). In the workplace, there are hundreds of decisions that are made every week. One person chooses method A, another person prefers method B. To keep the peace, we often have to defer to another's preferences.

I have a fantastic wife and a very good marriage. And we disagree on something almost every day! Linda and I have been married for 37 years. Linda is smart, hard working, funny, attractive and a devoted counselor to our children. She is always learning new things, devouring new books on everything from nutrition to education to business to midwifery.

She works as a midwife, caring for moms and babies and overseeing new births every month. For most of our kids' school years, she was their home-school teacher. You get the picture that she is very capable. She also has very strong opinions about a lot of things. When it comes to debating an issue, she's no pushover.

It's her right to disagree with me. We have learned how to have respectful, fair arguments. That means saying what we really think without anger, and trying hard to understand the other person's point of view. Most of the time, we stay within the boundaries of fair play. Sometimes our arguments escalate and get over-heated. But we have learned well the art of honoring one another and not letting bitterness take root. We don't hold grudges, even if there is some inflamed conversation along the way.

Laying down my life for Linda means I don't "insist on my own way."[183] This is one expression of humility. We forgive one another, knowing that the alternative would be deadly. I get a chance to serve Linda as Christ serves his church. What did Jesus do? He died for his bride. A startling depiction of what we are supposed to do. My job is to serve her. Whether it's marriage, church life or the marketplace, conflicts are part of life. Linda is a very generous and loving wife. We disagree because we are both human! So, I try to value her above myself. Sometimes, that means letting her win an argument even though I feel my viewpoint is justifiable.

Do we take Jesus' words at face value? Many of his words are very simple and direct, but not always easy to do: "Do to others as you would have them do to you."[184] How would I like to be treated? I want to be served and honored, of course! Hmmm, guess I can't get out of this one. I actually have to place others' needs above my own! The good news is, the Holy Spirit and the heart of the humble King is living inside us. Just go his way. As you lose your life, you find it!

Our job is to imitate Jesus, the gentle, humble King. He didn't just *tell us* what to do. He modeled it. Isn't it amazing that Jesus, through whom all worlds were made, was "humble and gentle of heart?" What a mystery—the Almighty God is humble and gentle.

God's character is multi-faceted. One way the Bible authors painted pictures of God was through animal metaphors. God is described as the "Lion of Judah." But he is also described as both a lamb and a dove. These are two of God's gentlest creatures. Jesus the lamb suffered death for our sake and the Holy Spirit in the form of a dove descended on Jesus at his baptism. "The lamb speaks of meekness and submissiveness and the Dove speaks of peace."[185]

Paul writes to Titus, "...be peaceable and considerate, and always to be gentle toward everyone."[186] I've had to work hard at overcoming my short temper. With eight children, I had plenty of learning opportunities. With a house full of kids, I often felt frustrated. When one of my kids did something wrong, I was tempted to command my children instead of gently speaking to them. I had to lay down my power, and lower the intensity of my voice and emotions. I made lots of mistakes, and slowly learned to be more gentle.

As parents, we have a powerful position over our children. As a husband, father and church leader, I can't have right relationship if I explode with anger. So I remember Jesus and surrender my power. Maybe you don't have a spouse or any children. But you have a few difficult coworkers in your office building or job site. All the same relationship principles apply to you as they do to spouses and parents. In the workplace, you can get your point across gently. You can use your authority without being bossy or pushy.

Humans disagree
In any gathering of people, there will be many different opinions about the right way to do things. We all have an opinion on every subject from what color to paint the walls to which songs to sing in church. Through church history, people fought over every imaginable doctrinal issue. That's one of the main reasons we have over 35,000 different church denominations in the world today.

It's simply human nature for us to have our own ideas. In the early church, people had a hard time working together! (It's no different today). In most of Paul's letters to the church congregations he pastored, he encouraged people to get along with one another, settle their arguments and forgive one another.

The examples of spiritual warfare in the New Testament are almost all tied to relational conflict. If the devil is messing things up, it usually starts in relationships. Here are two examples. To the church in Ephesus, Paul wrote: "Be completely humble and gentle; be patient, bearing with one another in love. Make every effort to keep the unity of the Spirit through the bond of peace."[187] Paul always addressed specific situations in his letters. He wrote this because they were not being humble and gentle, and their group was not always marked by peace.

A little further in chapter 4, Paul continues his line of thought, "Do not let the sun go down while you are still angry, and do not give the devil a foothold."[188] Discord in friendships is where the devil gets a foothold.

Paul wrote to the church in Philippi for the purpose of helping two key workers in the church settle an argument, "...in humility value others above yourselves, not looking to your own interests but each of you to the interests of the others."[189] "You don't always get what you want," John Wimber said to his pastoral staff one day. A simple but profound truth for all of life. If we could just let go of a sense of being *entitled* to get what we want, our lives would be more peaceful.

If I value someone *above* myself, I will shut up and listen to what they have to say. I will not only *listen*, but really consider what they are saying, trying to put myself in their shoes and see things from their viewpoint. The introduction to Paul's discussion of submission begins this way: "Submit to one another out of reverence for Christ."[190] Submit!? Yes, even in an age when our culture teaches us to "fight for our rights."

This isn't just a marriage issue, it's an *everybody* issue. This verse is attached to the previous paragraph that discusses being careful how we live, not getting drunk, and singing in church gatherings. It's amazing how strong people's opinions are about the "right way" to sing in church. It's one more opportunity to learn to humbly cooperate.

To submit means, "to give over or yield to the power or authority of another." That's what Jesus did. Easier said than done, but with the indwelling Holy Spirit we can do it. *Surrendering power* is a theme we see over and over again in the life of Jesus. For a good marriage, surrender your power. To win friends at work, surrender your power. Just as the two great commandments are intertwined and interdependent, "*love* God and neighbor," *submitting* to God and to one another go hand in hand. Love and submission must go in both directions—outward and upward. Each one leads us to the other.

Jesus "did not consider equality with God something to be used *to his own advantage*." You might have an advantage because you're good at arguing, or you're a powerful personality. Will you use that power to your own *advantage* or will you surrender your power?

Jesus teaches us what to do with our power
All of us have a sphere of influence— family members, coworkers, neighbors, and friends. We have responsibilities to do a job, care for people—as parents, employees, and church leaders. God gives authority in these relationships then he watches how we use that authority. As managers over a work force, we are tempted to "really let them know who is boss around here." Then we remember our servant King who chose not to lord it over his friends. He chose the humble road.

In the understanding of those who heard Jesus give the Sermon on the Mount, *blessing* was about inheriting the land, being taken care of and well fed. But Jesus gave them a new definition. Jesus said the "blessed ones" are those who surrender their power. One of the results of this kind of heart and behavior is that *we have peaceful relationships with those around us.*

"Blessed are the poor in spirit, for theirs is the kingdom of heaven."[191] *Poor in spirit* means an inner emptiness and humility and a readiness to learn. The poor in spirit are those who empty themselves of self-will. They aren't self-preoccupied or full of themselves. The poor in spirit don't compete with others to win spiritual or moral contests.

To be poor in spirit means you're not quick to argue, or get angry. The poor in spirit are willing to let the other person win the argument. The poor in spirit don't insist on their own way. They'd rather pursue peace than be the winner. When criticized, the poor in spirit don't retaliate. Instead, they seek peace. They seek the common good. They don't assume they have the most wisdom of anyone in the room.

In the desert temptation, Jesus didn't have anything to prove or protect. The Father protected him. "You are only free when you have nothing to protect and nothing you need to prove or defend."[192] Jesus let go of his rights to exercise divine power except as directed by his Father. "I always please my Father," he said. By yielding to the Holy Spirit who lives in us, we can exercise authority in a pure and gentle way for the good of others.

Tuning into the voice of the Holy Spirit isn't difficult. We simply empty ourselves of self-will and self-assertion and listen. Then we can tune into God's Spirit and wisdom. If we are teachable, we will learn and grow. The Holy Spirit will inspire us with *his* ideas.

In Jesus' Sermon on the Mount, he drills down to the root of division between brothers and sisters. He addresses the subject of *murder* and *anger*. Everyone knows that murder is wrong, but Jesus takes it much deeper to the underlying issue. He says that "anyone who is angry with a brother or sister will be subject to judgment." He wants us to root out our anger to foster unity and mutual love. Jesus says, "Lay down your power!" Paul echoes this sentiment in various of his letters, "Lay down your opinions and learn to get along with each other!"

Love is the answer
In the famous 13th chapter of Paul's First Letter to the Corinthians, Paul gives us the antidote for our selfishness. He describes what *love* really is. It's amazing how intertwined the characteristics of *love* are with the characteristics of *humility*.

Love is patient... I find it interesting that *patience* is the very first adjective Paul uses to describe love. To wait for other people to get out of your way in the kitchen or on the highway or in a conversation...requires

Living in Humility

that you *become small*. When you have to wait for another, you are not putting yourself first. Putting others *first* is a quick way to sum up, "Love your neighbor as yourself."

Love is not proud... Love is humble. These are two opposites. "God opposes the proud and gives grace to the humble."
Love does not demand its own way. Seeing others as better than yourself keeps you from demanding your own way.
Love keeps no record of being wronged. The humble naturally forgive, because they know they've been forgiven a huge debt.

Paul underscores the importance of love above all else: "*Let love be your highest goal*! What is your highest goal? Is it a successful career? A beautiful home? I have to keep reminding myself to make *love* my highest goal.

"*Lord Jesus, help us surrender our power like you did. Keep before our eyes the model of marriage that you give us in your word. Help us to submit to one another out of reverence for you, honoring one another above ourselves.*"

15

Be a Learning Machine

"It is impossible to begin to learn that which one thinks one already knows."[193] Epictetus

"Pride blunts the very instrument we need to own in order to succeed: our mind. Our ability to learn, to adapt, to be flexible, to build relationships, all of this is dulled by pride."[194] Ryan Holiday

"Abraham Lincoln...once said that he never met a person from whom he did not learn something, although most of the time it was something not to do. That...is learning, and it comes from your alertness."[195] John Wooden

One reason Jesus singled out little children as models of humility is that kids are learning machines. They have no choice but to learn. Everyone else is bigger, stronger, and knows more than they do. Being the "little guy" is the only thing they know, so they learn, learn, learn.

When we're no longer children, we like to pretend we know all we need to know. If there's something we don't know we are less apt to reveal our ignorance because we want to be seen as smart. To become great, as Jesus said, we have to resist that tendency, and become a learning machine. That's what humble little kids do.

Living in Humility

Children often say funny things. They have wrong ideas, and they get their words mixed up. But toddlers are usually OK with being wrong. They haven't learned to take pride in their knowledge, so they are open to instruction. Everyday, they have to be corrected and instructed by their parents.

To admit someone else knows more than you is to take a lower place. "The barrier during self-improvement is not so much that we hate learning, rather we hate being taught…it takes a lot of humility in order for one to fully develop."[196] Admitting we don't know all the answers is a tough choice, but it's the way to gain wisdom and honor: "Wisdom's instruction is to fear the Lord, and humility comes before honor."[197]

Be willing to try again after making mistakes
Jesus' disciples left everything to follow him. Having left all, they signed up to be in the 24/7 school of Jesus. The disciples made wrong statements, had wrong ideas and made wrong decisions all the time. But they kept learning.

When Jesus was multiplying the bread and fish, they had no clue what was happening. That's understandable. But after Jesus fed a group of 5,000 and another time fed a group of 4,000, they were still concerned about having no bread. They were very slow to catch on. But they made the choice to keep humbling themselves.

Jesus corrected them when they argued about who was going to be the greatest. He rebuked the disciples on several occasions for their unbelief. He corrected them when they were more excited about casting out demons than about being God's children. But the disciples hung in there as students of the Master. They were willing to admit they didn't know much.

When Peter first left his life as a fisherman to follow Jesus, he was impetuous and fickle. He is famous for three times denying that he ever knew Jesus. But, because he was teachable, he later became one of the most influential leaders in the early church.

Jesus was really good at showing the disciples their error, and giving them the next step in their training. Sometimes, people will be too polite to point out our errors. So we have to be our own best critic. And, because we all have blind spots, we should invite others to give us input. In the last few years, I've welcomed a few of my adult children to feel free to point out any bad behavior they see in my life. I don't want to stop improving.

"The humble person is open to being corrected, whereas the arrogant is clearly closed to it. Proud people are supremely confident in their own opinions and insights. No one can admonish them successfully: not a peer, not a local superior, not even the pope himself. They know - and that is the end of the matter. Filled as they are with their own views, the arrogant lack the capacity to see another view."[198]

My long-time friend, Gary Best, has traveled the world for many years to teach in conferences and churches. For much of his life, he served as a local church pastor and as the National Director for the Vineyard churches in Canada. He continues to speak in churches and also serves for a month per year at a ministry called St. Stephen's in Hong Kong along with his wife, Joy. St. Stephen's is a haven for many recovered drug addicts who have come to Christ, as well as a host of others.

Gary is an accomplished teacher but sees the value of being a father to younger leaders. While staying at St. Stephen's, he doesn't do a lot of teaching. He and Joy are simply available to spend time with leaders and workers who need care and encouragement.

The Bests are also involved in helping maintain the buildings on the campus of St. Stephen's, *Shin Mun Springs*. This complex of buildings is home for a few hundred people. One of Gary's tasks is to recruit and train people to repaint the apartment buildings.

Living in Humility

In his recruiting speech, Gary says, "I only want to train people who *don't* know how to paint." He knows that many of the brothers at St. Stephen's have had a tiny bit of painting experience. He knows that some of them consider themselves to be skilled painters even though their work is of poor quality. But there were some guys who were willing to learn from Gary from the very first step. Are you willing to become small and start from the beginning?

Lloyd Alexander wrote, "You must know nothing before you can learn something, and be empty before you can be filled. Is not the emptiness of the bowl what makes it useful?"[199]

The nine-time Grammy–and Pulitzer Prize–winning jazz musician Wynton Marsalis published his advice to developing musicians in a series of letters called *To A Young Jazz Musician*: Letters From The Road. Here is Marsalis' advice on staying in a learning mode: "Humility engenders learning because it beats back the arrogance that puts blinders on. It leaves you open for truths to reveal themselves. You don't stand in your own way. . . . Do you know how you can tell when someone is truly humble? I believe there's one simple test: because they consistently observe and listen, the humble improve. They don't assume, 'I know the way.'"[200] This attitude is essential no matter what skill you are learning—relating to family members, athletics, music, a building trade, or a medical profession.

In my late fifties, I started playing music a few times per month at an outdoor outreach event. The best way to fill this large outdoor parking lot with sound is with a full band. It was an opportunity for me to grow in my skills on electric guitar. I had dabbled in playing electric over the years, and wasn't very good at it. The acoustic guitar had always been my "go to" instrument.

I knew I had a lot to learn, so I started practicing. I didn't want to stay *stuck* using the wrong techniques. After many hours practicing and performing, I've learned a lot, and it shows in my performing. But I still have much to learn. I had to be honest with myself about my deficiencies as an electric guitarist before I was able to learn. No matter your age, you can keep learning and improving.

"We want to be done with learning. We want to be ready. We're busy and overburdened. For this reason, updating your appraisal of your talents in a downward direction is one of the most difficult things to do in life—but it is almost always a component of mastery. The pretense of knowledge is our most dangerous vice, because it prevents us from getting any better. Studious self-assessment is the antidote."[201]

Never stop learning
John Wooden, legendary basketball coach and author, wrote, "Learn as if you were going to live forever, and live as if you were going to die tomorrow...Always be learning, acquiring knowledge, and seeking wisdom with a sense that you are immortal and that you will need much knowledge and wisdom for that long journey ahead. Know that when you are through learning, you are through."[202] Wooden's blunt statement echoes the words of Proverbs: "Do you see a person wise in their own eyes? There is more hope for fools than for them."[203]

I'm sixty years old, but I'm a long ways from being *done!* I don't want to stagnate. I want to humble myself like a child and keep learning. Though you have gathered much knowledge, know that society is changing faster than ever before. Technology and social norms are evolving at the speed of light. Learn from those around you, including your children. I'm always picking up new information from my wife and kids because they are tuned in to new trends in society—in education, the arts, politics, etc.

Be aware of a tendency to hang onto old practices and patterns that aren't relevant. Keep learning; with the internet at your fingertips, researching any subject is easier than ever before. I remember the days when doing research was a big chore. Now I can do it on my living room couch with a laptop computer. Dig in and learn.

Living in Humility

An extraordinary learner

Kano Jigoro was a Japanese educator and athlete, and the founder of the martial art of Judo. Born in 1860, Kano had an extraordinary willingness to learn.

He modified the ancient martial art of Jujitsu, creating the art of Judo. Judo was then used by the Japanese police, and then was also accepted in the Olympic Games competitions. Kano found all kinds of ways for Japan to educate its youth in many different subjects. He was respected widely around the world for his contributions to athletics and education.

Right before his death, Kano asked all his students to gather around him for a visit. He gave them these instructions, "when you bury me, do not bury me in a black belt! Be sure to bury me in a white belt!"[204] In martial arts the white belt is worn by a *beginner,* a new student of Judo. Kano was reinforcing the lesson he had taught throughout his life—never stop learning! What a lesson in humility and teach-ability!

This reminds us to have the humble attitude of a child no matter how expert we may become. May we be eager to learn from those around us until the day we die.

16

Be A Team Player

I've always loved sports, both as a player and spectator. The value of participating in sports goes way beyond pure enjoyment. The hard work required to excel in sports forms our character. Learning good sportsmanship helps instill righteous virtues. In team sports, as in all of life, humility is essential.

My favorite basketball team is the Golden State Warriors. (Do I hear boos and cheers?) There are two main reasons I like the team. First, they have great players who are fun to watch. Second and most important, they have an amazing culture of unselfishness. Each player values the whole team more than he values his own rights. Humility is required.

One of the keys to their success is their passing game. Each player is quick to pass the ball to a teammate who is in a better position to shoot the ball instead of taking a risky shot himself. The statistics show they pass the ball more than any other team in the NBA. Selfish ego doesn't rule this team. By contrast, some star players from other teams are reluctant to let go of the ball. They might score a lot of points, but the team suffers. No team can reach its full potential if even one person is selfish with the ball.

Though there are several All-Star players with the Warriors, none of them are glory-hogs. Each one celebrates the success of the others, knowing there is one scorecard that really matters—the *team* score. A player who scores a lot of points catches the public's attention and will usually make more money. But the ethos of the Warriors' is *teamwork*, not individual stardom.

Stephen Curry is the Warriors juggernaut point guard who has broken all kinds of scoring records. "Stephen has reshaped the way basketball is played. He has been proclaimed the best shooter in basketball history and has the stats to back it up."[205] In the 2014–15 season, Steph led his team to their first NBA championship in forty years. He has twice been named the NBA's most valuable player. He's a devout Christian who is, "Likable, humble, soft-spoken, and living out his faith."[206]

Many players with his superstar status have a huge ego. Coaches who have to manage such arrogant players have an extra demanding job. On top of their regular coaching duties, they have to soothe the temperamental ego of the self-centered athlete. In 2018, the Warriors won another NBA championship. At the celebration dinner, Steve Kerr, the coach of the Warriors, forgot to say "thank you" to Steph Curry for his huge contribution to the team's success. But Kerr didn't worry about his oversight, because he knows Curry doesn't have an ego that needs to be constantly stroked.

Curry wasn't the least bit concerned that he didn't win the most-valuable-player award for the 2018 playoffs. He was quite happy for Kevin Durant, another elite player on the team, to garner this award. Curry isn't famished for people-praise because his goal is to please God. He gets his tank filled by receiving God's approval. He's not insecure—he knows that personal scoring statistics and human accolades aren't what really matter. It's a team sport. The team suffers defeat together, goes through tough times together, and celebrates the victories together. When the team wins, *everyone wins*.

Be a Team Player

Unity and unselfishness
The outstanding teamwork and self-sacrifice demonstrated by the Golden State Warriors is a great model for families, churches, and all organizations where people work together. Teamwork brings success, and it's also a lot of fun. Some of the Warriors have taken salary cuts of several millions dollars per year just to make room for other outstanding athletes to be added to the team. Not only do they want to be part of a *winning* team, they want to be on a *happy* team where everyone is valued and appreciated. Isn't that what we all want—to genuinely enjoy hanging out with our workmates?

One of the greatest basketball coaches of all time was John Wooden. For 27 years, Wooden coached at UCLA, my alma mater. Wooden retired the year before I began attending UCLA. His nickname was the "Wizard of Westwood." He won a total of ten national championships and led his team to a winning streak of 88 games in a row. Wooden was a man of integrity with a strong Christian faith.

Wooden was much more than a basketball coach to his players. He was a mentor who taught his players all sorts of lessons about the importance of strong character, habits and morals. Wooden created a diagram he called "The Pyramid of Success." This Pyramid identifies all sorts of qualities required for success in sports and in life, such as industriousness, friendship, loyalty, cooperation and enthusiasm. One of the values in this pyramid is *team spirit*. Says Wooden, "This means thinking of others. It means losing oneself in the group for the good of the group. It means being not just willing but eager to sacrifice personal interest or glory for the welfare of all."[207]

Members of one another
These are exactly the same attitudes and behaviors that unify the church, the family and any group of coworkers. In the body of Christ, we are joined together as one building, one family, and one temple of the Holy Spirit. We *belong* to one another. Every part of the body is a valued

Living in Humility

member and has a role in helping the other members. We weep with those who weep and rejoice with those who are doing well.

One of Wooden's favorite sayings was: "Consider the rights of others before your own feelings and the feelings of others before your own rights."[208] This is taken right out of Paul's letter to the Philippians. "...don't try to impress others. In humility, value others above yourselves...look to the interests of others."[209] Wooden recruited basketball players with unselfish attitudes: "I valued a player who cared for others and could lose himself in the group for the good of the group. A gifted player, or players, who are not team players will ultimately hurt the team, whether it revolves around basketball or business."[210]

In the body of Christ, no single individual should seek to be the brightest shining star. The only star is Jesus. In the Youtube age we live in, "impressing others" is way over-emphasized and overrated. As individuals, we are all part of a larger story.

No star status
Whether it's on a basketball team or in church, star status kills team unity. John Wooden explains his reasons for praising one star player and rejecting another: First Wooden describes the egotist, Dennis Rodman. "As great a player as Dennis Rodman is, and he *is* a great player, I wouldn't want him on a team. He is an egotist with a great desire to attract attention." Wooden, with his vast coaching experience, knew it would pull his team down to have a self-centered player like Rodman."[211]

In contrast, Wooden praised the attitude of Kareem Abdul-Jabbar, a record-breaking player for UCLA and in the National Basketball Association: "Kareem took his great ability to score and used it for the greater good of the team. He was willing to do that. But if either he or I had allowed that scoring ability to dominate, we would have cut down on the contributions of others to the detriment of the team. Kareem put the team ahead of himself."[212]

Be a Team Player

Will we help or hurt our team? To help a team, our family, our church, or our co-workers, we must value the group above ourselves. Humility is required. When someone else is "scoring huge points," on a sports team, church, or any kind of organization, the humble will rejoice, instead of being overcome by jealousy or self-pity.

Ancient Corinth—a magnet for the ambitious

New York City. What images come to mind when you think of this unique city? Wealth, fame, power, Wall Street, famous actors and singers, a place where people go to make their mark in life and to find success.

The ancient city of Corinth was similar to a modern day Hong Kong, London or New York City. It was a cosmopolitan city filled with people from many nations, cultures and religions. Corinth was a port city, situated by an isthmus on a heavily traveled trade route; commerce thrived there. Corinth was also a center for the arts and was also known for its sexual promiscuity, immorality, and heavy drinking. Ambitious people were drawn to this city to prove themselves and make money.

Paul came to Corinth in AD 50 to plant a church. Some of these smart, confident Corinthians discovered the gospel through Paul's teaching. The new converts brought all their issues of ego and ambition into the church. Before long, all kinds of problems developed, including arguing, division and the pursuit of special spiritual status. In their immaturity, they were out to prove themselves as elite Christians.

Paul begins his letter by affirming the Corinthian Christians for being enriched "with all kinds of speech and with all knowledge"[213] and for their spiritual gifts. Then he confronts their selfish ambition, arguments, selfishness and boasting. Paul shines a laser beam on their impure motives. He addresses the Corinthians as "people who are still worldly—mere infants in Christ...since there is jealousy and quarreling among you, are you not worldly? Are you not acting like mere humans?"[214]

He calls out their attitude of self-importance. It was a church full of wannabes—those who desperately want-to-be elevated above others. Paul redirects the Corinthians away from the pursuit of superiority towards humility.

Having worked in many churches, I know that people (including me) sometimes slip into competing with our own brothers and sisters for spiritual status. Just as in Corinth, worldly attitudes leak into the church. We find ourselves wanting to be the "star" instead of "passing the ball" to one another and encouraging others to shine. Godly ambition gone-wrong becomes selfish ambition.

In my career as a worship leader, I found selfish ambition to be like an ugly monster that had to be slayed again and again. When tempted to criticize and compete with other worship leaders, I tried to act in the opposite spirit. As Paul said to the church in Rome, "Do not be overcome by evil, but overcome evil with good."[215] When you're feeling jealous of others, bless them. Lift them up.

I've made a habit of sharing the platform with lots of other worship leaders, giving them opportunities to take my place. The more I've done that, the more I've slayed the dragon of narcissism and enjoyed the success of others. When it's in your power to give someone else an opportunity to shine, do it. Get really good at "passing the ball" to other players at your job and in the church.

Julius Erving and Moses Malone

Here's another standout story of attaining team unity and success through an attitude of humility. Pat Williams was the general manager of four different NBA teams in his career, and for the Philadelphia 76ers in the 1970s to 1980s. He recalls working with two of the most talented and humble basketball players ever. The first was Julius Erving—the legendary "Dr. J." He was one of the most celebrated athletes of his era.

Be a Team Player

Dr. J was a six-foot-seven forward, famous for launching from the free throw line and throwing down slam-dunks. Pat Williams says of Dr. J, "Despite his worldwide fame, Doc is the most humble and self-effacing athlete I've ever known—and the most confident. He epitomizes that all-important balance of confidence and humility that leads to success."[216]

Julius Erving joined the Philadelphia 76'ers in 1976 and rose to superstar status in the ensuing years. Several years later, the 76'ers hired Moses Malone, a six-foot-ten center with huge potential. While Erving had flash and style, Malone was a meat-and-potatoes center who muscled his way towards the basket and dominated opponents through sheer hard work and hustle. There was concern in the 76ers management about the compatibility of the two star players. Would the two players have the right chemistry to work well together? Or would Malone upset the 76ers winning combination of players?

Their concerns turned out to be groundless. When Moses was interviewed by a reporter on working with Julius Erving, he replied, "This is Doc's show, and it's always been a great show. Moses is just here to help Doc. And I think it's gonna be an even better show."[217] Because neither Malone nor Erving had a big ego, there was no clash between these two titans. In Moses Malone's first season, the 76ers won the NBA championship, and Malone was named playoffs MVP.

Pat Williams fondly remembers that year: "What we didn't realize at the time was that we were also hiring great humility. And it was that unbeatable combination of great talent and great humility that brought a championship to Philadelphia."[218]

Share your turf

Competitive people who lack humility are all about protecting their turf. "It's my team; I run the show." Instead of an attitude of teamwork, one-for-all and all-for-one, the egotist always has to be in control and in the spotlight. This elitist attitude was infecting the Corinthian church. The result of this competitive one-upmanship was disunity and broken relationships. Envy and jealousy were taking a toll. Paul's purpose for writing this letter was to uproot these toxic attitudes.

Paul uses the analogy of the human body to describe the church. Each person is compared to a part of the body with a unique function. Some of the Corinthians felt inferior among their peers, "Because I am not an eye, I do not belong to the body." In other words, they were saying, "I can't preach, I can't lead...I'm way too shy, untalented and unconfident." There were a lot of people feeling un-valued and left out in this church. They felt like they didn't belong because they didn't have outstanding spiritual gifts. But Paul is saying, "yes you *are* an important part of the body!"

Make everyone feel valued

In any athletic team, there are first string players who get the lion's share of game time. Some athletes get hardly any game time at all. Here is what John Wooden says about those players who may seem to be less valuable: "The individuals who aren't playing much have a very important role in the development of those who are going to play more. They are needed, and you must let them know it. Everyone on the team, from the manager to the coach, from a secretary to an owner, has a role to fulfill. That role is valuable if the team is to come close to reaching its potential."[219]

On a basketball team, the second and third string players work hard in practices, preparing themselves and preparing the first stringers by playing *against* them. Without a tough opponent in practices, the first team can't get ready. These unsung heroes that spend most of the games on the bench have a critical role. They are valuable.

Last season, as the Warriors were nearing another NBA title, I could see the sheer joy of the players on the bench. Though they were playing only a few minutes per game, this was *their* victory. They were just as much a part of this championship team as anyone. Everyone worked as hard as they could to contribute to the team's success.

Humility is to *accept the way God made you.* Humility is to *accept the opportunities God gives you.* Humility is to *rejoice when the super-gifted are shining.* Humility is to agree with God's sovereign distribution of gifts to his children. Wooden describes how we are all created uniquely and have differing opportunities: "Some of us are shorter or taller, quicker or slower, smarter or otherwise. Situations vary. Some people have more opportunities, some less. We are not the same in all these things, but we are all the same in having the opportunity to make the most of what we have, whatever our situation. The ultimate challenge for you is to make the attempt to improve fully and be your best in the existing conditions."[220]

All you can do is make the most of what God gave you. Accepting your limitations is a secret of contentment. When we catch this truth of God's sovereignty, envy and jealousy are crushed. Instead of envying, we appreciate others' gifts. St Augustine said, "Take away envy and what I have is yours too. And if I banish envy all you possess is mine!"[221]

It's about "us," not "me"

Paul reminds the Corinthian church of their corporate identity. He says, "we are coworkers in God's service; you are God's field, God's building…you together are the temple of the Holy Spirit."[222] Meditating on this truth is a sure-fire way to quell the spirit of selfish ambition: realize that you *belong* to the body of Christ. You are *members of one another*, as Paul says. You are part of a larger spiritual organism—the body of Christ. If you are a "finger" in the body, what you do on your own is just an extension of the arm, which is connected to the shoulder, etc. You can't take credit for anything on your own.

To those who in Corinth who had an air of superiority, Paul says, "The eye cannot say to the hand, "I don't need you!" We all need one another. We are called to include one another, help one another, agree with one another and honor one another. The person who can seemingly "do it all," must make love their highest goal, or they're no good in God's eyes.[223] Paul is saying, "It's not all about *you* as individuals, it's about the larger *you*, the whole body of Christ!" He says, "...What do you have that you did not receive? And if you did receive it, why do you boast as though you did not?[224]

Say 'no' to jealousy
God graciously sprinkles jewels of wisdom and talent on all kinds of people all the time. He doles out jewels of mental and spiritual gifting, artistic and athletic skill and great intelligence. We can look at these gifts in two ways: "I earned it and I'm taking credit for it" or "Wow, what a gift." If we see God as the giver of all good gifts, we see ourselves in the proper light. We can appreciate everyone as recipients of God's gifts—whether they be simple or extraordinary. Throughout my career as a worship leader and music artist, I've worked hard at buying into a team player attitude. I've had to put down my own ego over and over again. Competition is such a huge part of our culture. I have to fight against it and run towards the humble heart of Jesus.

The way of the world says, "Fight your way to the top. Personal performance is the only way to be rewarded." In the economy of God's kingdom, we find great reward in helping *others* rise up and find their place in our families, churches and businesses. He may give you outstanding personal success, and he may not. Embrace the larger story that surrounds you. Adopt God's definition of success.

"Give and it shall be given to you."[225] When you create a new opportunity for a child, you'll be rewarded. When you make room for a colleague or a friend to be recognized, you'll be rewarded. As you look for opportunities to lift up a young leader, as you give away your privilege to lead, God will give back to you in many ways. And you will gradually become more and more like your humble King.

17

God is at Work in You

"...Be energetic in your life of salvation, reverent and sensitive before God. That energy is God's energy, an energy deep within you, God himself willing and working at what will give him the most pleasure."[226]

"Who, me? Humble? Is that possible?" Does it seem ridiculous to entertain the idea that you could be called humble? Sometimes it does, to me. Until I remember that's who I really am, at the core of my being. The real me, in my spirit, is grafted into the very heart of Jesus. We have an ever-present teacher, patiently putting a hand on our shoulder to keep us from spitting out angry words.

Jesus said, "The Father and I are one."[227] He said, "Apart from the Father I can do nothing." The key for Jesus was being united with the Father and the Holy Spirit. We have that same union with God! If you know that Jesus is connected and united to you, you can rest. The same power that raised Jesus from the dead lives in you. The same heart of love and humility that drove Jesus to the cross is joined to your heart. Grace from heaven is constantly accessible to you and me.

Rest in your real identity in Christ

We are made in his image. As his Spirit-empowered children, we embody and reflect his traits. We have the capacity to think and act as Jesus did. As Paul wrote to the church in Corinth: "...we have the mind of Christ."[228] Jesus, full of grace, has made himself constantly available to us.

Without this understanding of your identity, you will be striving to climb an impossibly tall ladder to humility and godliness. Don't go climbing any ladders; just yield to the King inside you. When you make mistakes, like we all do, you'll feel hopeless and defeated unless you rest in the reality of being grafted into Christ.

If you oversee staff members or have children to raise, in a frustrating moment you will be tempted to pull a power play. You will feel like using the "big stick" of authority in the wrong way—with anger and aggression. In that moment, the Holy Spirit will help you remember, "Oh yeah, the real me is a servant." He will bring his thoughts to you, "Stop...think about it. What's your best choice at this moment?" God knows everything you need, sees everything you're doing, and resides in you! Boom! Divine power to do good is at your fingertips. The Spirit of humility, the Holy Spirit, is living inside of you, ready to enable and lead you every moment.

You embody the nature of Trinity

God has many attributes. One aspect of God's nature is humility. How could the almighty, ever-living God be humble? I don't know—it's one of those things that's beyond human comprehension. Two of the most docile creatures on earth are used to represent Jesus and the Holy Spirit—the *lamb* and the *dove*.

One of Jesus' titles is "Lamb of God." A helpless lamb. Jesus was the suffering servant, the humble King who left behind his privileged position at the right hand of the Father. Jesus always deferred to the Father. He chose to always please the Father. The Spirit of Jesus is one of humility. (Of course, he is also depicted as a lion, and he can "roar" whenever he wants to).

At Jesus' baptism, the Holy Spirit is depicted as a dove who descends onto Jesus. God is depicted as a gentle dove! The Holy Spirit defers to the Father and the Son. Jesus describes the Spirit's work: "he will speak only what he hears."[229] He is partnering with the Father and Son. God implants this readiness to respond to righteousness in us.

One of the Greek words that early church theologians used to describe the Trinity is kenosis, the act of self giving, or self-emptying, for the good of another. That describes a humble God. Not a hierarchy; more of a circle of love. The nature of Trinity shows us that God's power is not domination, threat, or coercion. All divine power is shared power and the letting go of autonomous power. If we yield to God-with-us, we will learn this humble posture.

Another word used in early church history to describe the Trinity is *perichoresis*, which means mutual submission or dynamic intermingling. This relationship has also been described as a dance. In Jonathan Marlowe's words: "There are not two dancers, but at least three. They start to go in circles, weaving in and out in this very beautiful pattern of motion. They start to go faster and faster and faster, all the while staying in perfect rhythm and in sync with each other. Eventually, they are dancing so quickly (yet so effortlessly) that as you look at them, it just becomes a blur. Their individual identities are part of a larger dance. The early church fathers and mothers looked at that dance (perichoresis) and said, "That's what the Trinity is like." It's a harmonious set of relationships in which there is mutual giving and receiving. This relationship is called love, and it's what the Trinity is all about. The *perichoresis* is the dance of love."[230]

The "mutual submission" that is described here is another word for humility. The Father, Son and Spirit bow to one another and cooperate in mutual love. We, as Spirit-born sons and daughters of God, contain the essence of this heart. As we nurture our bond with the Trinity and imitate their ways, we walk in the same kind of deferential humility.

United with the Holy Spirit

To the church in Colossae, Paul says: "For you died to this life, and your real life is hidden with Christ in God."[231] At the most core level of our being, we are "hidden with Christ in God." Paul says to the church in Ephesus, "But now you have been united with Christ Jesus."[232] The real you is a "partaker of the divine nature."[233] Don't buy the devil's lies that you are a dirty good-for-nothing. "My old self has been crucified with Christ. It is no longer I who live, but Christ lives in me. So I live in this earthly body by trusting in the Son of God..."[234]

If you have read scriptures like these hundreds of times, it's possible to gloss over the real meaning. If you have never been taught the real implications of being united with Christ then you'll miss it. You will see some kind of religious idea without the real power contained in that truth.

Most of Western Christiainity hasn't emphasized our union with Christ. Instead we have emphasized our individuality and separateness from God. As Thomas Merton wrote in his journal, "We are already one. But we imagine we are not. And what we have to recover is our original unity. What we have to be is what we already are."[235]

Put on Christ

We have unlimited capacity to be like Christ, based on his constant, powerful presence in us. He is in us; we just need to constantly "put on Christ" to realize and actualize his nature in our actions and words. We are fully connected to the Vine. The parable of John 15—the vine and branches—teaches us the completeness of this union.

Andrew Murray saw the power of this truth: "The branch, whether an original or an engrafted one, is such only by the Creator's own work, have no fear that you are far from him!"[236] It's not about how holy you feel! That's a relief! The Holy Spirit is not some capricious ghost! He's solidly with us forever.

Jesus grafted you, the branch, into himself, the vine. This is a very different picture than "God up there, somewhere." If God only resides "above all worlds" it's hard to picture him empowering me every minute of every day. The truth is, there is no separation between his Spirit and my spirit!

Constantly empowered to do all good things
"...the person who is joined to the Lord is one spirit with Him."[237] Knowing that you are one with the Lord causes faith to spring up like a beautiful fountain in your heart. Meditating on this truth makes you think, "I can do this." The gift of faith is working in you, empowering you to walk in love, kindness, and humility. Abiding in Jesus, your inner-partner, makes you willing to take out the garbage and clean up messes and not complain about it. He makes you willing to persevere through unimaginable difficulty. His and your purpose is to serve. Will selfish thoughts flood your mind? Of course! But that's not the real you. The real you wants to be completely humble and gentle and patient. Because his Spirit, his self, his essence, his power, his grace is joined to you.

It is about abiding, not performing
"None of us know how to be perfect, but we can practice staying in union, staying connected. 'Remain in me and I remain in you,' says Jesus. [238] It is about abiding, not performing. It is about holding to your core identity more than perfect behavior—which would only make you proud and self-sufficient—even if it were possible."[239] Trust him to do it! You are a branch connected to the Perfect Vine. If you clothe yourself with Christ and draw from his nourishing love and wisdom, you will bear his fruit.

Constantly nudged by the Holy Spirit—the Great Reminder

The humble always have an ear open to nudges from the Holy Spirit. Jesus said, "he will teach you everything and will remind you of everything I have told you."[240]

The Holy Spirit reminds you...
...not to insist on getting the royal treatment from people.
...to honor people around you who are in low positions.
...to look for ways to lift up the discouraged, destitute and exploited.

The Holy Spirit reminds you...
...to stop complaining because you don't have enough creature comforts...
...to let go of your rights instead of demanding your own way...
...that the best choice is to please the Father...

The Holy Spirit reminds you...
...that you can have peace even though you don't have everything figured out...
...what counts in the end; it's not earthly plaudits and praises, it's pleasing God with your life.

The mystical unity of the body of Christ

Each Christian's personal unity with God is hugely important. But there's another very important part of this big picture of Holy Spirit—connection. Just as there is a mystical union between the Lord and each of his followers, so there is a one-ness between the members of Christ's body, his church. "There is one body and one Spirit...one God and Father of all, who is over all and through all and in all."[241]

The same Spirit who indwells me also indwells you! He is our common bond. We are all connected. Paul tells us, "you are members of one another." "In Christ we, though many, form one body, and each member belongs to all the others."[242]

In this age of rugged individualism, "belonging to one another" is a radical view of our identity. God didn't call any of us to be an island. By the Spirit, we are one. That being true, we are to pursue intimate, connected relationship. We discover our unity as we choose to fellowship together and serve together.

"For we were all baptized by one Spirit so as to form one body—whether Jews or Gentiles, slave or free—and we were all given the one Spirit to drink."[243] We are the Spirit-connected organism called the church. We can access the Holy Spirit individually, and in a much more rich and diverse way as the corporate body of Christ. We are much more fully endowed with his gifts as the whole body than as solitary people. If we walk in humility, we will benefit from the wisdom, insight and gifts of the other members of the body.

The problem of broken relationships is one of the most common themes in all cultures and ages of human history. It is also one of the biggest problems in New Testament times and all throughout church history. Honoring our unity with Jesus and with one another makes it possible to foster relationships instead of losing them.

To the Philippians, who had a couple of leaders who were struggling to get along together, Paul writes: And this is my prayer: that your love may abound more and more in knowledge and depth of insight, so that you may be able to discern what is best..."[244] Paul is saying that love results in discernment.

As we live out our unity by loving one another, (which includes being humbly receptive and ready to learn from one another) we gain insight. Paul further encourages the Philippians towards unity, citing their *union with Christ* as the foundation for living in unity with one another:

"Therefore if you have any encouragement from being united with Christ...then make my joy complete by being like-minded... in humility value others above yourselves..."[245]

Being strongly connected to our church family is both a *resource* for individual growth and fruitfulness and a *challenge* to our selfish tendencies. Humility towards God and one another opens the door to all of God's resources for us.

He is in you

He is already in you. Talk with him and listen to him throughout your day. Absorb all of who he is. Live as his apprentice. Always be learning from him. And hang around others who act like him.

Cooperate with his transforming work in you. Constantly fill your mind with inspiring stories about what he has done. Listen to stories and teachings of his many followers.

"Imitate God," as Paul says. Slowly you will become more like him, thinking his thoughts, wanting what he wants and doing what he does. As you do that, people will notice something special about you because you carry the traits of love and humility. People will open up to you because you don't have an over-inflated view of your own importance.

He has no lack of resources for you! Humility is walked out by yielding continually to the abiding Spirit of Christ. This is the path of peace. Not a trouble-free life, but one of contentment.

If we allow God to be big in our lives, to keep increasing as we stay low, our lives will be full of joy and productivity. Thank God for this grace in which we now stand.

18

Growing Older Graciously

"The LORD brings death and makes alive; he brings down to the grave and raises up. The LORD sends poverty and wealth; he humbles and he exalts."[246] *1 Samuel 2:6-8*

Common to us all is the ever-marching process of aging. Whether you are 20 years old, or 70, it's so important to meditate on the way God set up his universe, and in particular, the brief human lifespan.

At the end of 2017, I reached the age of sixty—a big milestone. Time flies, and now I am technically past "middle age!" It naturally brings up a review and evaluation of life's lessons. As the years fly by, we think more about the inescapable truth: like all humans, one day we will die. The arrow is pointing towards your eventual death and the life to come. How will you handle it? How can you prepare for it? Graciously accepting the end of our earthly life is our last lesson in God's humility school.

Grumpy or grateful?

We've all seen grumpy old people in movies, books and real life. Now that I'm entering my seventh decade of life, I more acutely feel the pull towards being rigid, set-in-my-ways, and insistent on my long-held opinions. At the same time, I feel the tug of the Holy Spirit towards vulnerability, and teachability.

Living in Humility

Vulnerability is the way to genuine relationship. Again, Jesus showed us the way. He took a giant step downwards to become a human baby. He made himself subject to all the physical ills of earthly living—dirty diapers, searing hot weather, stormy seas, and parents who couldn't understand why their boy ran away to go to the temple. As the Servant King, Jesus knelt before those whom he created. He walked long distances on the dusty roads of Galilee and slept in all kinds of uncomfortable beds.

Why did he do this? He suffered extreme discomfort to build a bridge of relationship to the human race. He showed us how to find our life by losing it. At the end of his years with the disciples, he said to them, "As the Father has sent me, I am sending you."[247] He says the same to us.

The imperfect me is slowly being refined simply because I am a God-seeker who is around imperfect others. With a good dose of humility and love, I will progress. If I keep admitting my mistakes and learning from everyone around me, I have an opportunity to get better, instead of becoming bitter. If I can keep passing over the mistakes of others and accepting insults and injuries, I will progress. If I can keep my heart open and vulnerable in relationships, I will progress.

One way of stepping down and away from pride is to shun an attitude that says, "I deserve better than this." As a sexagenarian, there is a certain sense of entitlement I can succumb to: "After all, I'm 60 years old. Shouldn't I be treated with more respect?" Outside of North America, I've experienced more respect from younger people than I do in my home country. From what I've seen, respect and esteem for older people isn't the norm in North America. But that's no reason to complain. Consider Jesus, the highest ranking royalty of all, who never demanded royal treatment while on earth. Since Jesus is my model for living, I don't demand respect. Instead, I try to smile, wash the dishes and show kindness to those who marginalize me.

To shun the grumpy life, don't take yourself too seriously. Nicky Gumbel says, "The ability to laugh at yourself is key to holiness. Take Jesus seriously but don't take yourself too seriously. A sense of humor is the link between holiness and humility."[248] We take God very seriously. He is holy, perfect and all-powerful. We are like the flowers of the field, here today and gone tomorrow—like a mist that evaporates. At the same time we are his beloved kids. In a sense, we're all like 5-year-olds living in the safe and secure home of our generous Father. Standing next to God's greatness, how can we have an overblown opinion of our own importance? If we see ourselves with this perspective, laughing at our own foibles and limitations comes naturally.

Never forget that all of life is a gift—every year, every day, every moment is a gift. Every one of your natural talents, opportunities, and promotions in life are all a gift. You partner with God by developing your skills and walking through open doors, but it's all by his grace. There is no place for boasting. We are like kids who have been handed everything they need. Thinking about that sometimes makes me giddy with gratitude, and sometimes profoundly thankful.

This year around Thanksgiving time, I went for a walk and thanked God for all the blessings I could think of in my 60-year life. Everything from having healthy children and a wonderful wife, to having plenty of food to eat, to being surrounded by God's beautiful creation. Thankfulness and humility go hand-in-hand.

If you live in the United States, may I remind you that you are living in the wealthiest nation in the history of the world? (If you're in another first-world country, you're not far behind). You probably don't consider yourself to be rich, but the simple fact is that if you drive a car and have a little extra money in a bank, you are rich compared to most of the world's population. Since we're bombarded by advertisements aimed at convincing us that we don't have enough stuff, it's easy to forget that we live like kings compared to previous generations. I'm a grateful beneficiary of a hugely generous

Living in Humility

God. I've worked very hard, but the ability to work is merely a gift.

In the age of King David and his son, Solomon, the people of Israel generously gave money for the building of the temple. At the dedication of the temple, David prayed, "But who am I, and who are my people, that we should be able to give as generously as this? Everything comes from you, and we have given you only what comes from your hand."[249] We can only give back to him because he first gave to us.

It helps me to think of myself as an older version of my 5-year old self. When I was a kid, my parents chose to give me "allowance" money, and sometimes to pay me for doing chores. My parents were motivated by love, generosity, and a desire to train me to use my resources wisely. From that gift I could buy things for myself, give to the church or share with someone in need. It's the same now, except the dollar amounts are larger. My Father has been generous with me. Part of his generosity is allowing me to live in a nation and a time of history where most people have plenty. Pondering that truth engenders an attitude of gratitude, generosity and humility.

Adapting to the changing seasons of life

Looking back on my adult life, I see constant change for me and my family. I've had a continually evolving job description, I've lived in many different cities, and my children have grown from babies to adults. Changes like these can be exciting but are often uncomfortable and upsetting. The comfort of old patterns, such as having small children around and the predictability of a regular household routine, are gone. My wife, who was a stay-at-home mother for 25 years, now works outside of the home. To keep thriving, I have to humbly accept the new landscape of my life with gratitude and trust. "Blessed are the flexible, for they shall not be broken" is something I heard Chuck Smith say in a sermon—a good modern day proverb for anyone.[250]

Thinking about the shortness of life on earth

In an earlier chapter I quoted John Wimber's statement: "The Way In is the Way On." We could add to that, "The Way In is the Way *Out*." We came into this world as helpless humble babes. We came into Christ's love by humbly bowing, and we will leave this world in the same posture.

Think about the trajectory of your life in the positive light of God's big plan. A limited time on earth for each of us is God's healthy design. Everyone will die, but people avoid discussing it. If we really believe we'll be resurrected with Jesus, death shouldn't be a depressing topic. Thinking about "the end" is not a macabre or morose practice – it's wise. The beginning of your life is a gift from God and so is the end. Wonderful things await you in the next life. Thinking about the next life of "reigning with Him" is intriguing and encouraging.[251]

Accepting the brevity of life on earth is one of the many ways we bow to God. Each one of us is part of that broad brush of God's painting of human history. He has ordained it: "There is a time for everything...a time to live and a time to die."[252] So, we humbly yield to his design for our lifespan.

Socrates, the famous philosopher who lived 400 years before Christ, died an unjust death in prison. He was a social and moral critic. He argued for justice and goodness and opposed the oppressive power of the government. His views irritated the politicians, poets and artists in ancient Greece. They felt he wasn't honoring the Greek gods. When Socrates was in prison facing imminent and unjust death, his jailers, some of the cruelest men in the land, mocked him and asked, "Why do you not prepare yourself for death?" He looked at the jailers and replied, "I have prepared for death all of my life by the life I lived." In this statement, Socrates echoes biblical teaching: "LORD, make me to know my end and what is the extent of my days; Let me know how transient I am."[253] "So teach us to number our days, that we may present to You a heart of wisdom."[254]

Living in Humility

The long arc from birth to death

If you were like most babies, you were born healthy. You grew bigger and stronger through many years of healthy growth. Each year, you gained more knowledge and all kinds of life skills. In your twenties, you still had almost boundless energy. In early adulthood, most of us feel good (especially if we eat right and exercise). Sadly, some are struck with illness or accidents despite all their best attempts at healthy living.

In your thirties, you are in the prime of life but your body begins a very slow process of going downhill. At this stage, you still have plenty of strength and stamina, but you don't have quite the endurance you once did. In middle age, your body isn't quite as beautiful as it once was...your face looks older, you may gain weight and lose muscle mass. You lose your youthful look. You have more aches and pains, and you grow tired more quickly. Your vision and hearing slowly weaken. At this stage of life, the truth of our mortality becomes more of a felt reality. We can practice healthy living, but we can't stop the aging process, no matter how many nutritional supplements we take. In middle age, we come to grips with letting go of any attachment to our physical appearance.

Looking in the mirror and seeing an "older person" forces us to think about eternity. It's an in-your-face reminder that the unseen things are more important than physical things. It's a reminder to live for the eternal things. "Set your minds on things above, not on earthly things."[255] Think about the city that is to come: "For here we do not have an enduring city, but we are looking for the city that is to come."[256]

The inner person, the spiritual part of us, is what's going to live forever. Paul says to the believers in Corinth, "One day 'these bodies of ours' will be 'taken down like tents and folded away, they will be replaced by resurrection bodies in heaven'"[257]

Many years ago, one of my relatives said to me as she watched her much older husband approach death, "Old age is not for the faint of heart."

We have to prepare for the end of our lives. God has provided plenty of wisdom to help us get ready. I'm daring to believe that with God's help I will be able to peacefully and gratefully navigate the coming years, or decades. As King David said to God, "My times are in your hands."[258]

What to do with the rest of your life

The average life span has increased dramatically in the last 100 years. In a survey conducted a few years ago measuring life expectancy in Canada (where I live), women are living an average of 84.1 years, and men, an average of 80.2 years. By comparison, in the year 1919, the average lifespan in the United States for women was 56, and for men, 53. When you reach your 60s, 70s and 80s, what will you do? I look forward to spending time with my kids and grandkids, but I'll do much more than that. My plan is to continue to use what I've got to help others. We need to ask ourselves, "what impact am I having that will outlast my own life?"

One of my little ways of sharing my gifts is to play worship music at a meal for the poor in my community. Volunteers from more than 40 churches help put on a nightly dinner for the needy with a Christian organization called *Nightshift*[259]. Joined by a few other musicians, I play music in an outdoor parking lot where the meal is served. The servers tell us regularly that the worship music changes the atmosphere and the moods of the guests, and that the spirit of worship makes it much easier to talk to the guests, who can be angry and close-minded much of the time. From my vantage point on the platform, most people aren't paying attention to the band. They're eating and chatting with one another. But I can see some people receiving the peace and truth of God, and sometimes swaying with the music. This is a small example of the discipline of serving, of intentionally taking time to honor people who have a tough lot in life.

The story of Ruby

Here's a true story from the ministry of Steve Sjogren, author and former Vineyard pastor. Steve met a lady named Ruby from his church who was in her 70s. Ruby was in poor health. The doctors weren't giving her much time. Steve felt urged to challenge her, "If you only have a little time left, why not use it to serve others like there's no tomorrow?"

The next Saturday, Ruby went with a servant evangelism team to care for single moms and pray for the sick. On the outreach, Ruby prayed for a woman in her 90s who hadn't been able to flex her ankle in many years. When Ruby prayed, she could move her foot! Ruby took a step of faith, despite her own weakness and frailty. Faith is spelled R-I-S-K, even in your 70s and beyond.

The last third of your life is a time to be thankful for all the blessings you've received. Don't get into self-pity. Fight the good fight of faith by thanking God for every blessing you can think of—your family, friends, church, daily bread, and for all the spiritual blessings he has showered on you. Thank him for creating you, saving you, and for being your best friend.

Don't let cynicism get the best of you. Have people hurt you? Of course they have. Everyone gets hurt in life. Don't let that rule you. When you remember a painful memory, forgive as you've been forgiven. Humility dissolves anger and heals old wounds. Don't let your heart be hardened.

We can't love or be loved unless we're vulnerable. Pride and pessimism push people away, while humility welcomes them. "Some people may have one hundred children and live a long life. But no matter how long they live, if they aren't content with life's good things, I say that even a stillborn child with no grave is better off than they are."[260] Be content! Remember Jesus, who was sinless yet suffered terrible treatment from people. He surrendered to his Father's will. Imitate his humility.

My aim is to always be thankful: "Let my whole being praise the Lord! I will praise the Lord with all my life; I will sing praises to my God as long as I live."[261] Is there something standing between you and thankfulness? To praise God in spite of life's difficulties requires humility. It requires letting go of your right to have everything you want.

Your most fruitful years?

In some ways, when you're in your 60s and beyond, you have more to offer than ever before. You have accumulated a huge amount of life experience. You've learned thousands of lessons through trial-and-error. You're not as big a knucklehead as you used to be! "In old age is wisdom; understanding in a long life."[262] The latter part of your life is a time to pass along everything you can to the generations that follow: wisdom, experiences, practical help, and money. It doesn't matter how old my children are, I try to keep giving to them.

Though you have gathered much knowledge, you can share it only with people who want to listen! Aha! Another opportunity to grow in humility! Most of the time, you have helpful ideas to pass on to your grown children. But your teenagers and adult children have a limited appetite for hearing your opinions.

"Dwell in the land and do good."[263] Simply do good, (just like Ruby). Do good to your family, your church, and your community. Sweep floors, do dishes and give your adult children a break by taking care of their children. Do simple acts of service that lift a burden and relieve stress for someone else. Join Jesus in his upside-down kingdom—take joy in doing the grunt jobs. It's all Jesus stuff. In giving away our time and energy, we get our eyes off our own problems and find more peace.

Remember the "change in God's pocket" metaphor. Happiness is found in being spent by Jesus—nickels and dimes of God's love poured out. Joy is found in throwing yourself into serving others. One of my favorite examples of this is the work of Jimmy Carter, former US president, in Habitat for Humanity. Habitat for Humanity is devoted to building simple, decent, and affordable housing for the poor. They have addressed issues of poverty housing in many different countries.

Jimmy and Rosalynn Carter became involved as high-profile proponents of Habitat for Humanity in 1984. They have been involved in fund-raising and publicity as well as actual homebuilding. They have spearheaded projects supporting the Gulf Coast community seeking to rebuild after hurricanes Katrina and Rita in 2008, and in several Southeast Asian countries in 2009. After holding the highest position in U.S. government, Jimmy Carter asked God, "What's next?" and did something very practical to help people.

Saving up for your kids

Paul talks about saving his own money so he can travel to Corinth for a visit: "Now I am ready to visit you for the third time, and I will not be a burden to you, because what I want is not your possessions but you. After all, children should not have to save up for their parents, but parents for their children." [264]

Paul is setting an example for older fathers and mothers in the faith. Older people with resources should naturally be watching for younger ones who need help. If you have the wherewithal to pay your own way on a ministry trip to some country or church that needs your help, consider doing it. Maybe your "ministry trip" is to tutor people at the local elementary school. Maybe it's to the local retirement home. Maybe it's to fly across the country to help your own kids.

Embrace the short trajectory of your life with joyful expectation of what's around the corner. Know that God is good, and that his earthly and heavenly plans for you are good. Prepare for the end of your earthly life with faith and expectation. Make the most of your time on earth and keep growing in God on the second-half downward slope of your earthly arc.

"Little me, big God...look at all these great blessings you've given me that I haven't earned. You are so great, I am so small. You are so strong, I am so weak. Help me always be grateful. I bow before you."

19

Staying on the Humble Path

"Life is a long lesson in humility." Sir James Matthew Barrie

"The world tells us to seek success, power and money; God tells us to seek humility, service and love." Pope Francis

How to sum up *Following the Humble King?* Looking back on four decades of faith and anticipating the future, here are my thoughts on walking life's long road with humility.

In choosing Jesus, we are automatically enrolled into his Lifetime School of Humility. Following and imitating Jesus naturally leads to greater humility. As long as we diligently follow the humble King, we don't have to invent ways to become more humble. There are plenty of hurdles and collisions on life's road that invite us into choosing humility over pride. With faith, love and humility, there is a way forward that is full of hope and peace.

God's Humility Lesson Plan has many chapters. As I watch my young adult children grapple with the challenges of finding meaningful work and providing for themselves, I remember how difficult that period of life was for me. Graduating from adolescence into adulthood is fraught with challenges. But the toughest of times can be packed with God-encounters.

Living in Humility

Navigating the uncharted waters of adulthood is a refining crucible that brings spiritual growth if we keep diving into God's heart. In my late teens and early twenties, I grew by leaps and bounds in knowing God because it was my first experience of hanging onto him for dear life. He was refining me and lifting me up as I became his eager student.

Humility is essential when you're 26 years old and God hasn't yet opened the door for you to work in your chosen field. Humility is essential when you're a 35 year-old married woman who still hasn't been able to conceive a child. Humility is required when you're 47 years old and you are let go from a job position you've held for 21 years.

We all have "I didn't ask for this" moments in our lives. In those moments, the humble heart says to the Lord, "You're the potter, I'm the clay. Make me and mold me."

Get Jesus, get wisdom and humility

In his chapter on the destructive nature of our fiery words, James writes, "Who is wise and understanding among you? Let them show it by their good life, by deeds done in the *humility* that *comes from wisdom*."[265] James tells us that gaining *wisdom* produces *humility*. Jesus is the *Logos*, the *word of God*. He is our wisdom. In seeking Jesus, we gain wisdom, which produces humility. James describes true heavenly wisdom as, "pure, peace-loving, considerate, submissive, full of mercy and good fruit, impartial and sincere." This list of heavenly-wisdom-traits is basically a description of humility! Being humbly wise is synonymous with being a Christ-follower. Again, we see the foundational nature of the virtue of humility.

Jesus had many practical humility habits. After his resurrection he was exalted as *conquering* King, but on earth he walked as the humble King. He never manipulated people. He respected their freedom of choice. He was ready to respond to blind beggars by the side of the road and didn't resist a sick woman who desperately grabbed his robe to receive healing. He accommodated crushing crowds of hungry people who needed help. He was always listening to his Father for instructions, deferring to him at all times. He never abused his amazing spiritual gifts. If we keep doing the main-and-plain Jesus stuff, we'll be in good shape.

Love, friendship and letting go

The older I get, the more I value friendship—with God, and all kinds of people. The humble experience friendship with God. Two outstanding facts about Moses are his humility and his face-to-face conversations with God. I believe that friendship with God and humility are interdependent. Moses' humble heart opened the door to those conversations. He was eager to hear the Lord speak. In Psalm 25 we read, "The LORD *is a friend* to those who fear him"[266] or "The Lord *confides* in those who fear him."[267] Our "fear" of the Lord is best described as reverential awe and respect offered by his beloved children.

The humble and expectant heart is depicted in this picture from Psalm 123: "We keep looking to the LORD our God for his mercy, just as servants keep their eyes on their master, as a slave girl watches her mistress for the slightest signal."[268] God is a fountain of wisdom, and he is always ready to speak and reveal himself to those who reverently wait for him—in any place, at any time. He may not speak to us "face to face" (yet) like he did with Moses, but he will consistently whisper his words of wisdom to the hungry, humble heart.

The Christian life is a paradox

You receive by giving, and you become great by serving. Only in laying down your life do you find your life. Those who humble themselves will be lifted up. Jesus, the lamb who suffered for us and was exalted to God's right hand, is humble. It's no surprise that he calls us to walk the same humble road. The faithful who are granted long lives on earth run a marathon of learning to imitate the Humble One. He takes us from glory to glory, and we can enjoy all things if we let go of everything!

An example of that is Paul's instruction to the Corinthians. The culture of the immature Corinthian church was one of grabbing for prominence instead of living humbly. When they were arguing about which sub-group of their church was the greatest, Paul said to them, "All things are *yours*, whether Paul or Apollos or Cephas or the world or life or death or the present or the future—all are yours, and you are of Christ, and Christ is of God."[269]

To this group who had a serious case of FOMO (*fear of missing out*), Paul was saying, "Let go of your lust for notoriety so you can really enjoy life. Don't try to force your way into the forefront. Instead, humble yourself and let God bless you." As soon as the Corinthian believers let go of self-exaltation, they could appreciate the other leaders and their followers instead of clashing with them. Letting go of having your own way is the key to friendship with people and with God.

The more we embrace being linked to others in a community of faith, the more joy we receive from seeing others shine. Paul says to the self-centered Corinthians: "Do not be conceited."[270] He was teaching them about looking outward; about the paradox of receiving by giving. When our life is not about being the star of our own movie, we can appreciate the other characters. It's not just my story, it's my friends and family and faith community, all under the big umbrella of the salvation story.

Freedom in being bound to Jesus
Rabindranath Tagore was an Indian poet, musician, writer and artist who was born in 1861. He began writing poetry as a young child and in his lifetime produced thousands of poems, songs, novels, short stories, paintings and sketches. Widely known in his home state of Bengal, he is sometimes remembered as the "Bard of Bengal."

Tagore used the example of a violin string to portray the paradoxical nature of freedom. "I have on my table a string," wrote Rabindranath. "It is free to move in any direction I like. If I twist one end it responds; it is free.

But it is not free to sing. So I take it and fix it into my violin. I bind it and when it is bound, it is free for the first time to sing."[271] Just as a violin string produces beautiful music when bound to the instrument, so we can make beautiful music when we are united with Jesus, our humble King. We find our real purpose in life only when we are moving in sync with his desires, held in place by his righteous laws and boundaries. We find freedom in imitating Jesus or being "bound" to him. Only then can our life sing the same song Jesus did—a song of love and humility.

I will leave you with one final picture that describes humility. In the Ancient Near East, there was a custom of bowing to one another as a form of greeting. Greeting a guest by bowing was an, "expressive custom of saluting with the head erect and the body a little inclined forward, by raising the hand to the heart, mouth, and forehead. The symbolic meaning of this action is to say something like this: "My heart, my voice, my brain are all at your service."[272] May that be our constant attitude to God.

Lord, we bow to you. We are at your service. We offer you our hearts, voices, brains, and strength. Thank you, Jesus for your humble example and your constant empowering grace and intimate friendship. Help us to represent you to the world around us.

Notes

Chapter 1

William Bernard Ullathorne, *Patience and Humility,* Sophia Institute Press, 1998.
[2] Andrew Murray, Humility, fig-books.com, 2012, page 185.
[3] Thomas à Kempis, The Inner Life.
[4] James 4:6, Common English Bible

Chapter 2

[5] Maia Szalavitz, Humility: A Quiet, Underappreciated Strength, Time Magazine, April 27, 2012
[6] Ibid.
[7] 1 Corinthians 15:10, New Living Translation.
[8] Proverbs 11:2, English Standard Version
[9] Proverbs 3:34
[10] Psalm 25:9, Psalm 147:6
[11] Psalm 149:4
[12] Daniel 10:12
[13] Proverbs 22:4, New International Version
[14] Andrew Murray, Humility, fig-books.com, 2012, page 218.
[15] Matthew 11:29, New Living Translation.
[16] Andrew Murray, Humility, fig-books.com, 2012, page 85.

Chapter 3

[17] Richard Rohr's Daily Meditation, Daily Devotional from the Center for Action and Contemplation
[18] Ruth Haley Barton, Strengthening the Soul of Your Leadership, InterVarsity Press, 2008, page 47).
[19] Philippians 2:3,4, New International Version
[20] Matthew 3:17, New International Version
[21] 2 Co 1:8, 9a, New International Version
[22] 2 Co 1:9b, New International Version
[23] Deuteronomy 8:3
[24] See 1 Cor. 10:11
[25] Jay Pathak, sermon given at Mile High Vineyard Church, Denver, Colorado.
[26] Romans 12
[27] Jay Pathak, sermon given at Mile High Vineyard Church, Denver, Colorado.
[28] Matthew 4:3,4, New International Version
[29] John 3:30, King James Version
[30] Richard Rohr's Daily Meditation, Daily Devotional from the Center for Action and Contemplation

Chapter 4

[47] Luke 19
[48] Matthew 4:23, New International Version
[49] Leviticus 6:1-7
[50] Exodus 22:4
[51] Luke 7
[52] Matthew 5:39, New International Version
[53] Jared Boyd, message given at Langley Vineyard, October 2017
[54] John 14:9

[55] Micah 6:8
[56] Luke 1:28, Common English Version
[57] Daniel 8:27
[58] Luke 1:32, The Message
[59] Luke 1:34, The Message

Chapter 5

[60] Lk 1:38, New International Version
[61] Ruth Haley Barton, Strengthening the Soul of Your Leadership, InterVarsity Press, 2008, page 80).
Dom Humbert van Zeller, *Holiness for Housewives: and Other Working Women*, Sophia Institute Press, Manchester, New Hampshire, 1951.
[63] *Luke 1:46-48,* New International Version
[64] Rich Nathan, from a sermon at the Vineyard Church in Columbus, Ohio
[65] Madeleine L'Engle, A Circle of Quiet, Harper San Francisco, 1972.

Chapter 6

John Wooden, Wooden: A Lifetime of Observations on and off the Court, page 10, McGraw Hill, 1997, page 10.
[67] Gayle D. Erwin, The Jesus Style, Yahshua Publishing, 1983.
[68] Heidi Baker and Rolland Baker, Learning to Love: Passion, Compassion and the Essence of the Gospel, Chosen Books, 2013.
[69] By Stephen Marche, The Atlantic Monthly, May 2012.
[70] Mother Teresa, No Greater Love, New World Library, Novato, California, 1989, page 27.
David Brooks, The Road to Character, Random House, New York, 2015, Page 52.
Greg Paul, God in the Alley, WaterBrook Press,

Colorado Springs, 2004, page 14.
[73] Ibid, page 16.
[74] Ibid, page 17.
[75] Ibid, page 31.
[76] Greg Paul, page 24.

Chapter 7

[77] Frances Perkins, Wikipedia,
[78] https://en.wikipedia.org/wiki/Frances_Perkins
David Brooks, The Road to Character, Random House, New York, 2015, page 44.
[79] Ibid, page 44.
[80] Ibid, page 92.
[81] Robert Coles, Dorothy Day: A Radical Devotion (Da Capo Press, 1989), 115.
[82] Brother Lawrence, The Practice of the Presence of God, PracticeGodsPresence.com, 2002.
[83] Ibid.
[84] Ibid.
[85] Ibid.

Chapter 8

John Wooden, Wooden: A Lifetime of Observations on and off the Court, McGraw Hill, 1997, page 146.
[87] Nikki Gumbel, Bible in One Year, www.bibleinoneyear.org.
[88] Nikki Gumbel, Bible in One Year, www.bibleinoneyear.org.
[89] John 8:29, New International Version
[90] Romans 2:29, New International Version
[91] John 12:43, New International Version
[92] David Brooks, The Road to Character, Random House, New York, 2015, page 189.

[93] Augustine, Confessions, translated by Rex Warner. New York: Mentor, 1963.
[94] Galatians 6:9, New International Version
[95] Matthew 6:1, New International Version
[96] Revelation 22:12, Contemporary English Version
[97] Genesis 15:1, New International Version
[98] Psalm 19:7,8
[99] Proverbs 12:14
[100] Revelation 19
[101] 2 Timothy 2:12
[102] 2 Corinthians 4:17
[103] Deuteronomy 25
[104] 1 Samuel 15:12
[105] Gayle D. Erwin, The Jesus Style, Yahshua Publishing, 1983.
[106] 1 Samuel 15:24, New International Version
[107] 1 Samuel 15:30, New International Version
[108] Psalm 33
[109] Hebrews 11:6, New Living Translation

Chapter 9

[110] Rick Warren, from a sermon at Saddleback church, California.
[111] Andrew Murray, Humility, fig-books.com, 2012, chapter 8.
[112] C. S. Lewis, Mere Christianity, HarperCollins Publishers, New York, 1952, page 125.
[113] John Calvin, Institutes of the Christian Religion
[114] Psalm 139:23-24, The Message
[115] 1 Samuel 15:17, New International Version
[116] 1 Corinthians 1:18, New International Version
[117] 2 Corinthians 11:30, New International Version
[118] see 2 Corinthians 11:16-21
[119] Dallas Willard, Renovation of the Heart, NavPress, Colorado Springs, 20012, page 107.

[120] 1 Timothy 1, New International Version
[121] Romans 11, New International Version
[122] Ryan Holiday, Ego is the Enemy, Portfolio / Penguin, New York, 2016, page 73.
https://bygosh.com/nonfiction/autobiography-of-benjamin-franklin/a-letter-to-samuel-mather/ and http://www.masshist.org/database/533

Chapter 10

[124] Psalm 37:3, New International Version
[125] Psalm 37:7, New International Version
[126] Proverbs 20:24, New International Version
[127] Gen 12:1, New Living Translation
[128] Gen 15:1, New International Version
[129] Gen 13:17, New International Version
[130] Genesis 17:1, New International Version
[131] Psalm 37, New International Version
[132] Romans 12:14, 17, 21, New International Version

Chapter 11

[133] Nelson Mandela, Conversations With Myself, Anchor, Canada, 2010, page 406.
[134] Jim Collins, HarperCollins Publishers, 2001, page 30.
[135] Ibid, page 27.
[136] Ibid, page 21.
[137] Ibid, page 17.
[138] Ibid, page 18.
[139] Ibid, page 27.
[140] Ibid, page 29.
[141] Ibid, page 29.
[142] Pat Williams, Humility: The Secret Ingredient of Success, Shiloh Press, 2016.

[143] Proverbs 11:14, The Message.
[144] Jeff Boss, 13 Habits Of Humble People. Forbes Magazine, Mar 1, 2015.
[145] Ibid.
[146] Ibid.
[147] Jim Collins, Good to Great, page 29.
[148] Maria Bartiromo, The Ten Laws of Enduring Success, Crown Business, 2010, page 24.
[149] Ibid.
[150] Ibid.
[151] Pat Williams, Humility: The Secret Ingredient of Success, Shiloh Press, 2016, page 37.
[152] CS Lewis, Mere Christianity, HarperOne, 1952, page 33.
[153] Pat Williams, Ibid.
[154] Philippians 2:15, New International Version
[155] Proverbs 22:4 New Living Translation

Chapter 12

[156] Pope Francis, A Big Heart Open to God, HarperOne, 2013, page 59.
[157] Jeffrey A. Krames, Lead with Humility, American Management Association, 2015, page 44.
[158] Pope Francis, A Big Heart Open to God, HarperOne, 2013, page 31.
[159] Matt. 9:12, New Living Translation
[160] John 1:46, New International Version
[161] Luke 2:24
[162] Luke 4:14, New International Version
[163] Luke 4:18, New International Version
[164] 2 Co 8:9, New International Version
[165] Luke 7:22, New International Version
[166] Luke 10:28, New International Version
[167] Mother Teresa, No Greater Love, New World Library, Novato, California, 2002, page 22.

[168] Jorge Mario Bergoglio and Abraham Skorka, On Heaven and Earth, Penguin Random House, pg 229.

Chapter 13

[169] Proverbs 17:9, The Message
[170] J.K. Rowling, Harry Potter and the Half-Blood Prince, Bloomsbury Children's Books, 2014, page 137.
Pat Williams, Humility: The Secret Ingredient of Success, Shiloh Press, 2016.
[172] Ibid.
[173] Ibid.
[174] Proverbs 16:32, New Living Translation
[175] John Ruskin www.goodreads.com/author/quotes/1606.John_Ruskin
[176] Matthew 5:5, New International Version
[177] See Matthew 18
[178] Matthew 5:38
[179] Brené Brown, Daring Greatly, Penguin Random House, 2012, page 34.

Chapter 14

[180] Andrew Murray, Humility, fig-books.com, 2012.
[181] 1 Peter 5:5, New International Version
[182] Andrew Murray, Humility, fig-books.com, 2012.
[183] 1 Corinthians 13
[184] Luke 6:31
[185] Roy Hession and Revel Hession, http://biblehub.com/library/hession/the_calvary_road/chapter_5_the_dove_and.htm
[186] Titus 3:2, New International Version
[187] Ephesians 4:2,3, New International Version
[188] Ephesians 4:27, New International Version
[189] Philippians 2:3,4, New International Version

[190] Ephesians 5:21, New International Version
[191] Matthew 5:3, New International Version
[192] Richard Rohr, Daily Meditation, from the Center for Action and Contemplation. (cac.org)

Chapter 15

[193] Epictetus, Discourses and Selected Writings, Penguin Books, page 258.
[194] Ryan Holiday, Ego is the Enemy, Portfolio / Penguin, New York, 2016, page 74.
[195] John Wooden, Wooden: A Lifetime of Observations on and off the Court, McGraw Hill, 1997, page 184.
[196] Criss Jami, Killosophy, copyright 2015 by Criss Jami
[197] Proverbs 15:33, New International Version
[198] Thomas Dubay, Fire Within, Ignatius Press, San Francisco, page 188
[199] Lloyd Alexander, The Remarkable Journey of Prince Jen, Puffin Books; Reprint edition, 2004.
[200] Wynton Marsalis, To A Young Jazz Musician: Letters From The Road, Random House, 2005, page 11.
[201] Ryan Holiday, Ego is the Enemy, Portfolio / Penguin, New York, 2016, page 39.
[202] John Wooden, Wooden: A Lifetime of Observations on and off the Court, McGraw Hill, 1997, page 30.
[203] Proverbs 26:12, New International Version
[204] Wayne Cordeiro, Attitudes that Attract Success, Regal Publishing, 2001.

Chapter 16

[205] Mike Yorkey, The Right Steff, Shiloh Run Press, 2016, back cover.
[206] Ibid, page 11.

[207] John Wooden, Wooden: A Lifetime of Observations on and off the Court, McGraw Hill, 1997, page 188.
John Wooden, Wooden: A Lifetime of Observations on and off the Court, McGraw Hill, 1997, page 198.
[209] Phil 2:3-4, New Living Translation
[210] John Wooden, Wooden: A Lifetime of Observations on and off the Court, McGraw Hill, 1997, page 74.
[211] Ibid, page 78.
[212] Ibid, page 78.
[213] 1 Corinthians 1:5, New International Version
[214] 1 Corinthians 3:1,3, New International Version
[215] Romans 12:21, New International Version
[216] Pat Williams, Humility: The Secret Ingredient of Success, Shiloh Press, 2016, page 215.
[217] Ibid, page 218.
[218] Pat Williams, Humility: The Secret Ingredient of Success, Shiloh Press, 2016, page 219.
John Wooden, Wooden: A Lifetime of Observations on and off the Court, McGraw Hill, 1997, page 139.
[220] Ibid, page 171.
[221] Nicky Gumbel, Bible In One Year online daily devotional.
[222] 1 Corinthians 3:9, New International Version.
[223] See 1 Corinthians 13
[224] 1 Corinthians 4:6-7, New International Version.
[225] Luke 6:38, New International Version.

Chapter 17

[226] Philippians 2:12b-13, The Message
[227] John 10:30, New Living Translation
[228] 1 Corinthians 2:16, New International Version
[229] John 16:13, New International Version

[230] Jonathan Marlowe, https://jorgeschulz.wordpress.com/tag/jonathan-marlowe/
[231] Colossians 3:3, New Living Translation
[232] Ephesians 2:13, New International Version
[233] 2 Peter 1:4, English Standard Version
[234] Gal. 2:20, New Living Translation
[235] Thomas Merton, Orbis Books, Maryknoll, New York, 2000, page 140.
[236] Andrew Murray, Humility, fig-books.com, 2012
[237] 1 Cor. 6:17, New Living Translation
[238] (John 15:7).
[239] Richard Rohr, Daily Meditation, from the Center for Action and Contemplation. (cac.org)
[240] John 14:26, New Living Translation
[241] Ephesians 4:4, 6 New International Version
[242] 1 Corinthians 12:5, New International Version
[243] 1 Corinthians 12:13, New International Version
[244] Philippians 1:9,10, New International Version
[245] Philippians 2: 1-3, New International Version

Chapter 18

[246] 1 Sam 2:6-8, New International Version
[247] John 20:21, New International Version
[248] Nov 10, Nikki Gumbel, Online Bible in One Year.
[249] 1 Chron. 29:14, New International Version
[250] Chuck Smith was pastor of Calvary Chapel in Costa Mesa, California.
[251] 2 Timothy 2:12
[252] Ecclesiastes 3:2
[253] Psalm 39:4, New American Standard Bible
[254] Psalm 90:12
[255] Col 3:2
[256] Heb. 13:14, New International Version
[257] 2 Co 5:1–2, The Message

[258] Ps 31:15
[259] Nightshift Street Ministries, see nightshiftministries.org
[260] Ecc. 6:3, Common English Bible
[261] Ps 146:1,2, Common English Bible
[262] Job 12:12, Common English Bible
[263] Ps 37
[264] 2 Co 12:14, New International Version

Chapter 19

[265] James 3:13, New International Version
[266] Psalm 25:14, New International Version
[267] Psalm 25:14, New Living Translation
[268] Psalm 123:2, New Living Translation
[269] 1 Cor 3:21-23, New International Version
[270] Rom. 12:16, New International Version
[271] October 31, Nikki Gumbel, Online Bible in One Year.
[272] www.bible-history.com, *Manners and Customs*

Made in the USA
San Bernardino, CA
15 January 2019